M

THREE PLAYS

The new authorized English translations

by MICHAEL DEWELL

and CARMEN ZAPATA

Introduction by

CHRISTOPHER MAURER

———

Farrar, Straus and Giroux

New York

FEDERICO

GARCÍA LORCA

THREE PLAYS

BLOOD WEDDING

—

YERMA

—

THE HOUSE OF

BERNARDA ALBA

Library of Congress Cataloging-in-Publication Data
García Lorca, Federico, 1898–1936.
[Plays. English. Selections]
Three plays : Blood wedding, Yerma. The house of Bernarda Alba /
Federico García Lorca ; the new authorized English translations by
Michael Dewell and Carmen Zapata ; introduction by Christopher
Maurer. — 1st ed.
p. cm.
Translation from Spanish.
I. Dewell, Michael. II. Zapata, Carmen. III. Title.
PQ6613.A763A226 1993 862'.62—dc20 91-44203 CIP

11 13 15 14 12

The translators dedicate their work

TO MARGARITA GALBAN
—*for asking them to do it*

TO NINA FOCH
—*for believing they could*

TO CHRISTOPHER MAURER
—*for making it so much better*

Contents

Introduction by Christopher Maurer / *ix*

BLOOD WEDDING

I

YERMA

107

THE HOUSE OF
BERNARDA ALBA

189

Translator's Note / *291*

Music / *293*

Introduction

These three plays are often referred to as a "rural trilogy" and as García Lorca's most mature and characteristic works. *Blood Wedding* (first performed in early 1933) and *Yerma* (1934) were, in fact, intended as the first plays in a "trilogy of the Spanish earth," but that trilogy was never completed. *The House of Bernarda Alba* (finished in 1936; performed and published posthumously) does not form part of a cycle. Lorca was assassinated, at the age of thirty-eight, two months after he finished *Bernarda Alba*, and had no chance to meditate upon the final configuration of his works.

Although these plays have long been considered classics of the modern European theater, Lorca himself regarded them as the works of a beginner. As he worked on *Bernarda Alba*, which he had no opportunity to polish into a final draft, he told a Spanish journalist:

> . . . *I still consider myself a true novice, and I'm still learning my profession* . . . *One has to ascend one step at a time* . . . *[One shouldn't]* demand of my nature, my spiritual and intellectual development, something that no author can give until much later . . . My work has just begun.*

Nor did Lorca consider these plays to be especially "characteristic" of his own labor. Since 1920, the year of his first theatrical production (a fable about insects entitled *The Butterfly's Evil Spell*), he had experimented incessantly, both cultivating traditional genres (the puppet play, the historical drama in verse, farce) and challenging them. At a critical moment in his development as a dramatist he would identify two early experimental plays, *The Public* (begun in 1930) and *Once Five Years Pass* (finished in 1931), as more truly *his* than the rest of his works. He said that he had written his other plays, including *Blood Wedding* and *Yerma*, "in order to show [my] personality and to earn respect" within the mainstream theater. Such comments were meant to remind the public that his theater had already taken off in other directions, that he hoped to go on breaking new ground, and that he was *not* to be classified as a writer of "folk tragedies."

There was widespread agreement in the 1920s that the Spanish theater was undergoing a deep crisis. A stream of books and newspaper articles deplored the mediocrity of playwrights, the ignorance of critics, actors, and audiences, and the indifference of government officials. Few writers were more aware of this crisis than Lorca. In 1929, from his dormitory room at Columbia University, where he was working on *Poet in New York*, he wrote to his parents: "One must think of the theater of the future. Everything that now exists in Spain is dead. Either the theater changes radically, or it dies away forever. There is no other solution."

In 1929 Lorca had not yet become famous as a playwright. Only two of his plays had been performed and he was chiefly known as the author of *The Gypsy Ballads* (1928). What he brought back from New York, where he went often to the theater, was a sense of urgency and perspective, and the feeling that he himself could help to revitalize the Spanish stage. It was in America that he began work on *The Public* (never performed during his lifetime), a drama which calls for the abolition of conventional theater.

In fact, the Spanish stage was far from "dead," and reform was well under way. Two writers, Miguel de Unamuno (1864–1936) and Ramón del Valle-Inclán (1866–1936), had protested indignantly, earlier in the 1920s, against the banality of Spanish theater, and both were to leave a deep impression on Lorca. The ascetic Unamuno tried to strip text and stage of unnecessary ornament and to explore the same problems he had confronted in his philosophical essays and novels: artistic creation, faith, free will, personal identity. Calling for a return to the austerity of classical tragedy, Unamuno had rewritten the myths of Medea and Phaedra, and had struggled without success to find a modern expression for dramatical fate. In *Yerma*, a play where, as Lorca once remarked, "nothing *happens*," one feels Unamuno's disgust with a theater, and nascent film industry, dominated by "squirrelish action," as well as his insistence on emotional intensity.

More prolific and influential than Unamuno, Valle-Inclán experimented with re-creating Shakespearean tragedy and with new forms of tragicomedy. The greatest of Valle-Inclán's later plays grow from the simple intuition that what seems tragic to some (a spouse's infidelity, for example) is often regarded by others as comical or grotesque. Lorca develops that perception in two of his farces: *The Shoemaker's Prodigious Wife* and *The Love of Don Perlimplín for Belisa in Their Garden*. There are occasional verbal echoes of Valle-Inclán's works in Lorca's poems and plays, and Valle's trilogy *Comedias bárbaras* contained three elements that deeply interested the younger playwright: their rural setting; their use of theatrical space; and their peculiar vision of tragedy. Like Lorca, Valle-Inclán had the eye of a painter with a keen sense of space and color. Both writers set many of their plays not in aristocratic salons or drawing rooms but in a highly stylized Spanish countryside. Valle-Inclán was an implacable enemy of mediocre actors, and he must also have impressed Lorca by his refusal to compromise with the commercial theater.

Another aspect of Valle-Inclán's work seems relevant here: his fascination with melodrama. Arguing that Spaniards had a penchant for shouting, Valle-Inclán wrote his dialogue in fragmented, exclamatory language, and drew ironically on the melodramatic tradition of José Echegaray (1832–1916) and others. Unlike Lorca's, his intentions were satirical. But there is more than a hint of melodrama in Lorca's own theater, especially in *Blood Wedding*, the very title of which harks back to Echegaray.

Neither Unamuno nor Valle-Inclán had the artistic gifts or practical skills he needed to *realize* his vision and produce his works successfully. The multi-faceted Lorca was able to draw costume designs and stage settings, to arrange music for his plays, and even, on occasion, to accompany the actors at the piano. He also trained himself thoroughly as a stage director and supervised rehearsals and performances. In New York he had come into contact with amateur theater groups and professional repertory companies. A year after his return to Spain, with the end of the Primo de Rivera dictatorship and the declaration of the Second Spanish Republic (1931), he was able to form such an amateur group himself, attract government funding, and use the experience as an apprenticeship in theatrical production. His travels with La Barraca, a troupe of student actors who gave free performances of classical Spanish theater for rural audiences, forced him to grapple with practical problems of stagecraft, the training of actors, and the adaptation of classical works. This experience also led him to consider two closely related questions which concerned him deeply throughout his life: the impact of theater on society and the needs and expectations of different sorts of audiences.

A deep concern for social justice is evident even in Lorca's earliest works. But no doubt the trip to New York (his first encounter with urban masses) and the social turmoil of Republican Spain brought that concern to the fore. There is hardly anything in *Blood Wedding* that might be construed as social criticism, but by 1935 Lorca had declared himself an "enthusiastic, devoted follower of the theater of social action," and defined theater as

a school of laughter and lamentation, an open tribunal where the people can introduce old and mistaken mores as evidence, and can use living examples to explain eternal norms of the heart . . . The theater is an extremely useful instrument for the edification of a country, and the barometer that measures its greatness or decline. A sensitive theater, well oriented in all its branches, from tragedy to vaudeville, can alter a people's sensibility in just a few years, while a decadent theater where hooves have taken the place of wings can cheapen and lull to sleep an entire nation.

When Lorca attacks the norms of theatrical realism and the expectations of middle-class audiences, one senses that, emboldened by Surrealism, he is questioning not only an aesthetic current but certain aspects of urban, bourgeois morality: its supposed indifference to suffering, its hostility to deviant forms of behavior, its fear of death and of the forces of nature, its mistrust of fantasy, of dream, and of the artistic imagination. *Blood Wedding* had won almost universal praise for having restored tragic poetry to the Spanish stage, but *Yerma* was harshly criticized by the right-wing press as a subversive attack on "decency" and traditional Spanish values. *Bernarda Alba* was not performed during Lorca's lifetime, but its very subtitle, "Drama of Women in the Villages of Spain," suggested a critique of the status of women in male-dominated Spanish society. An introductory note declares that *Bernarda Alba* is intended as "a photographic documentary." Other projects on controversial social themes, from homosexuality to pacifism, were in preparation when Lorca was murdered in Granada in August 1936.

Poetry and Music

There are two areas in particular in which Lorca's theater differs radically from that of his predecessors: his idea of poetic drama and the musical nature of his works.

"Theater," Lorca remarked in 1936, is "poetry that rises from the book and becomes human enough to talk and shout, weep and despair." In Lorca's work, drama and poetry seem inseparable. His poetry often has the dramatic quality that he admired in traditional Spanish songs and narrative ballads, and his drama has the metaphorical density, the attention to rhythm, the ring of "memorable speech" one normally associates with poetry. In each of these plays, images, metaphors, and symbols form a coherent whole, a poetic system whose full meaning cannot be paraphrased.

The distinction between prose and verse was not an essential part of Lorca's aesthetic. Form and genre often seem almost accidental, a means to an end. On occasion, he describes prose pieces and even drawings as "poems." *Yerma* is proudly subtitled "A Tragic *Poem* in Three Acts and Six Scenes." Without ever theorizing about poetic drama, Lorca knew that it did not necessarily entail the use of verse. It was, simply, drama written by poets ("The theater which has endured has always been that of poets"). That guiding ideal, which bore its first fruit in *Blood Wedding*, was unprecedented in Spanish theater. No Spanish playwright since Lope de Vega or Calderón de la Barca had appealed so forcefully to the poetic imagination of so many people, from such a wide cross section of society, in Spain and abroad. None has done so since Lorca's death.

In the 1920s and 1930s the Spanish theater was not entirely friendly to what Lorca understood as poetic drama, but it was remarkably tolerant of verse. Historical drama, for example, was still being written in verse by Eduardo Marquina (1879–1946) and others. Lorca himself had contributed to this tradition in *Mariana Pineda* (1927), the story of a woman executed in Granada, in the early nineteenth century, for having taken part in a liberal conspiracy against the tyrannical Ferdinand VII. What was unusual and revolutionary in Lorca's later plays was the use of both prose and verse within the same work, as in *Blood Wedding*. No major Spanish writer since Romanticism had combined the two so boldly and gracefully. In *Blood Wedding*, Lorca once remarked, prose and verse have their own distinct functions:

Well-wrought, free prose can soar to expressive heights, freeing us from the confinement and rigidity of meter. Let us welcome verse at moments when the excitement and disposition of the theme demand it, only then. You can see that, in Blood Wedding, *verse does not appear with any intensity or at any length until the wedding scene. Then, with the scene in the forest and in the last scene in the work, it takes complete command of the stage.*

The use of verse decreases in *Yerma* and is almost entirely absent from *Bernarda Alba*, where María Josefa's lyrics acquire special intensity because they interrupt the "prose" of the other characters. As he worked on *Bernarda Alba*, Lorca told a friend that it had "not a single drop of poetry." But, arguably, the last two dramas are no less poetic then *Blood Wedding*. Together they are an important part of Lorca's challenge to Western theater: the sense that, in our own age, "poetic theater" need not be written in verse, be at odds with realism, or remind us of the theater of the past (none of these plays sounds at all archaic in Spanish).

The American critic Francis Fergusson, one of the first to recognize Lorca's achievement, noted in 1957 that Lorca "wrote poetic drama, very much as Yeats and Eliot have taught us to understand it; yet his plays are neither cultish nor middlebrow-

Erstaz: they are theater-poetry which lives naturally on the modern stage." Although he was familiar with Eliot's *The Waste Land*, Lorca does not seem to have followed the dramatical experimentation of either Eliot or Yeats, and he never theorized about theater poetry. "The greater the poet," he once remarked ingenuously, "the greater his theater."

The second distinctive characteristic of Lorca's theater is music. As a young man, he had studied the piano and had tried his hand at composition. A few of his early pieces are preserved in the Fundación Federico García Lorca, Madrid. It was only after the death of his piano teacher in 1916 that he turned from classical music to literature. His enduring passion for music—folk, popular, classical, contemporary—was nurtured in the 1920s by Manual de Falla, a close friend of the Lorca family, with whom Federico wrote the text of an unfinished comic opera (*Lola, the Actress*), and by other composers, performers, and musicologists of Lorca's own generation: Adolfo Salazar, Ernesto Halffter, the guitarists Andrés Segovia and Regino Sáinz de la Maza, the dancer and singer Encarnación López Júlvez, "La Argentinita."

Not surprisingly, both in his poems and in his plays Lorca tries to reconcile literature and music, at first by using musical imagery (e.g., "the fermata of the half moon") and later by drawing on musical structures, as in *Suites* (1921–23), a book of poetic sequences several of which take the form of a theme and variations. As stage director and as a writer of dialogue Lorca is also aware of the crucial importance of rhythm:

One needs to rehearse for a long time, and very carefully, to achieve the rhythm that ought to govern the performance of a dramatical work. To me, this is very important. An actor cannot wait a second too long before opening a door. A flaw of this sort has a deplorable effect. It is as though, when one were interpreting a symphony, the melody, or some other musical effect, were to come in at the wrong time. The hardest thing to achieve in the theater is to have the work begin, develop, and end in accordance with an established rhythm.

Lorca's vision of theater draws upon ballet and other forms of dance, and as a director he devoted much attention to the stylization of movement. In 1933, on staging a series of Spanish popular songs in Buenos Aires, he spoke of the need to devote more attention "to the human body, which is completely forgotten in the theater. We must present a festival of the body, from the toes . . . to the hair. Ruling over all this we have the actors' eyes, indicating what is going on inside them. The body, its harmony, its rhythm, has been forgotten . . . We must restore value to the body in the theater. That is what I am trying to do."

Nowhere is musical form more apparent than in *Blood Wedding*, where the characters' speech is "orchestrated" in a highly stylized, rhythmic manner that sometimes borders on liturgical chant. Lorca's brother, Francisco, who wrote brilliant essays on each of these plays, has remembered how concerned the poet was about the rhythm of Act II, scene I, where the Bride leaves for the wedding: literally, "let the Bride awaken / on the morning of the wedding." That scene, he writes, is "fragmented by many characters entering and leaving, at different heights on the stage, with the alternating play of male and female voices, speaking lines of extraordinary rhythmic complexity. Federico interrupted the rehearsals frequently, exclaiming, 'It has got to be mathematically precise.' " The actress Josefina Díaz de Artigas, who played the Bride in the 1933 Madrid premiere, remembers that Lorca staged that scene rather like the conductor of an orchestra, "so that there wouldn't be a single voice that didn't blend with the others . . . He combined the voices, their special timbres and strengths, as a composer puts together sounds. It was an extraordinary effort. He would shout, 'Not you! Your voice is too shrill! *You* try. I need a deep voice. I need a fresh voice here.' "

There is ample textual and biographical evidence suggesting the preeminence of music in Lorca's theater. For example, in a production of *Blood Wedding* in New York during Lorca's lifetime (1935), lines assigned to the Mother and the Wife in the final scene are interchanged, as though characterization mattered less than tonal harmony. The translator, who consulted frequently with Lorca, noted on his manuscript: "Federico thinks that, instead of Novia [the Bride], the womenfolk like a choir should speak these words. But he did not dare to do so in Madrid, on account of poor work of second-rate actors."

We know, in addition, that as Lorca wrote the play, during the summer of 1932, he listened obsessively to two records: one of *cante jondo* singer Tomás Pavón, and one of a Bach cantata. Though it is impossible to identify that cantata, it is tempting to suppose that the wedding scene in *Blood Wedding* was inspired in part by cantata no. 140 (*"Wachet auf! ruft uns die Stimme"*), a joyful celebration of the symbolic marriage of the daughters of Jerusalem with Christ:

"Wake up," cries the voice of the sentinel from his tower. "Wake up, O Jerusalem!"

What we hear in the cantata, writes W. G. Whittaker (and his words are equally relevant to *Blood Wedding*), is "an amazing scene of excitement and confusion, people rushing to and fro, sounds of voices coming from all quarters of the streets, while the serene and divine announcement of the coming of the Bridegroom peals above the mêlée" (*The Cantatas of J. S. Bach, Sacred and Secular*). Lorca is working with dramatical components somewhat analogous to those of the cantata. In Act II, scene I, of *Blood Wedding* we find choral and individual singing as well as short, spoken prose passages. In the first movement of the cantata, the sopranos' call, *"Wachet auf!,"* is repeated by the altos, tenors, and basses. García Lorca's strikingly similar refrain ("Let the Bride awaken / the morning of the wedding") is sung and spoken by different men, women, and children, in a sort of imitative entry. Not surprisingly, the cantata has been compared to a theatrical work:

The accompanying voices are lively, psychologically apt, and at one point . . . even impatient with the slow pace of the hymn tune. The accompanying voices will do most of their energetic urging-on in carefully spaced bursts of fervor. As if this were a mass scene on the theater stage, Bach changes the order of their mostly imitative entrances as often as possible. [Gerhard Herz, ed., *Cantata No. 140, Wachet auf! ruft uns die Stimme*]

No less important than the rhythmical stylization upon which Lorca insisted as director are two other musical elements: the songs and dances performed by the characters, and the background music. The songs of the washerwomen in *Yerma* or the spinners in *Blood Wedding* are reminiscent of Spanish folk tunes. They are also meant to suggest the choruses of Greek tragedy, commenting on the action and revealing something of the psychology of the characters. "What interests me most about my drama," Lorca said of *Yerma*, "is the process of [Yerma's] obsession. She speaks the same way, from when she enters until she leaves, and I have taken care to accompany her with a monotonous musicality."

Lorca also used music as a way of weaning his audiences from expectations of realism. What he says of the music in his farce *The Shoemaker's Prodigious Wife* is applicable also to *Blood Wedding*: "The use of music allows me to make the scene less realistic, and do away with the audience's impression that what is going on is 'really happening,' permitting me to raise things to the level of poetry." There is a good example of this technique at the beginning of Act III of *Blood Wedding*, where the stage directions are: "A forest. Night. Great moist tree trunks. A murky atmosphere. Two violins are playing." It is not known what music those violins are playing, but a translator's note in the manuscript of the New York production reveals what the audience listened to in Madrid, in 1934, as it waited for that act to begin: "Andante of Brandenburg Concerto of Bach. They used a disk in Madrid. It has to sound from afar. When curtain rises, the Three Woodcutters are on stage, without moving." Presumably, this would have been the andante from the Second Brandenburg Concerto. Remembering two different moments in the play, Lorca later remarked that "*Blood Wedding* . . . is taken from Bach . . . That third act, the scene in the woods, the moon, the business of death prowling around: all this is in the Bach cantata that I had." Few plays are more thoroughly musical than *Blood*

Wedding; several recent stage and film versions dispense entirely with the text.

Tragedy and Elegy

In the wake of Unamuno and Valle-Inclán, but in a profoundly original way, Lorca declared his intention to "return to tragedy. Our dramatical tradition obliges us to do so." For Lorca, tragedy entails certain formal elements (the chorus, for example), but above all it involves creating an illusion of fate or destiny, of "necessariness": the suggestion that men and women are at the mercy of elemental forces which shape their lives in ways they barely comprehend. For Lorca, tragedy is woven from the "necessary" speech of poetry (the illusion that there is *no other way* to express what is being said) and from "necessary" action (the illusion of destiny). This feeling of inevitability must be coupled with mystery ("Only mystery makes us live," Lorca wrote beneath one of his drawings). In his view, no tragedy can be fully explained. For him, the very essence of poetry and tragedy lies in mystery, and the mystery of his plays is not generated by abstract ideas or by suspenseful action but by the resonance and ambiguity of his poetic imagery: imagery firmly rooted in the senses. Lorca's images flee from abstraction and seem to arise from material reality. Emotions, for example, are often expressed as physiological phenomena:

How can it be that something as small as a pistol or a knife can destroy a man who is like a bull? I'll never be quiet. The months go by, and the desperation stings my eyes and the very tips of my hair!

. . .

Every time I mention her, I feel as if I'd been struck in the forehead with a rock.

Yerma's solitude finds expression in simple images like these:

I want to drink water, and there's no glass and no water! I want to climb the hill, and I have no feet! I want to embroider my petticoats, and I can't find the thread.

Leonardo describes what he felt when the Bride married another man:

> *The silver pins of your wedding*
> *Were making my blood turn black.*
> *And dream was filling my flesh*
> *With bitter, choking weeds!*

Water and weeds, hill, pins, thread . . . however mysterious its meaning, Lorca's imagery arises from what can be seen, touched, smelled, or heard. "A poet must be a professor of the five bodily senses," he once observed in a lecture on Góngora. Throughout Lorca's theater, general ideas like fate or death become almost tangible.

There is also, as Francisco García Lorca has noticed, a movement in the opposite direction. As with the characters, whose "generic" names remind us that they are eternal types, particular objects—a horse, an arm, the knife, the moon—come to seem universal, essential, prototypical. While searching for the Bride, the Bridegroom remarks:

See this arm? Well, it is not my arm—it is the arm of my brother and of my father and of everyone in my family who is dead! And it has so much power that it can pull this tree up by the roots if it wants!

This movement from the particular toward the universal helps produce an illusion of tragic fate. Tragedy involves a search for the essential, eternal quality of things, as in the Maid's stunningly simple definitions of marriage: "It's a shining bed! And a man! And a woman!" Or the Mother's: "One man, some children, and a wall six feet thick to shut out everything else." Or Bernarda's view of the sexes: "A needle and thread for the woman; a mule and a whip for the man." This is a world of "men that are men, wheat that is wheat," where things recover their essences.

For all its sensual immediacy, Lorca's imagery makes a bold appeal to the subconscious. Deploring the sober rationalism and "objectivity" of modern American poetry, Robert Bly writes:

"Lorca's poems have many things in them sharply observed ('black doves puttering the putrid waters'), but they also have images, also passion, wild leaps, huge arsenic lobsters falling out of the sky." Lorca does not delve into the subconscious in the manner of Freud, as did other Spanish playwrights of the 1920s, and 1930s, or in the manner of the Surrealists. He draws on magical thinking which often resembles that of ancient naturalistic religions. Such "magic" is everywhere in *Yerma*. Conception, for example, is no scientific matter; it is something breathed into the ear, or something that fills the voice, or something drawn from the earth: "Many nights I go out on the patio—barefoot, to feel the earth under my feet—and I don't know why." The religious historian Ángel Alvarez de Miranda has studied many of these primitivistic elements: the overwhelming presence of the moon, as giver and taker of life; the deeply felt images of blood and of water; the ritual veneration of the knife; etc.

In his search for what is tragic and essential Lorca drew skillfully on a millennial tradition. He liked to imagine Andalusia as a historical palimpsest of pre-Roman, classical, Christian, Jewish, and Islamic elements. All three of these tragedies allude, as well, to contemporary events, altered and re-created by the poet. *Blood Wedding* has its origin in a newspaper account of a murder committed the day before a wedding in Níjar, in the southeastern province of Almería, and it is Almería, where cave dwelling is not unknown, which suggested the arid landscapes of that play, "hard as a landscape on an inexpensive ceramic piece." There are numerous "factual" details in *The House of Bernarda Alba*: an Alba family lived near the García Lorcas in the Andalusian village of Asquerosa, and, not surprisingly, some of the characters in the play—Bernarda, Poncia, and others—were suggested by real people. And yet, as happens in Lorca's poetry, modern elements like these are transformed credibly into something very ancient. The fertility rites in *Yerma* are based partly on the yearly pilgrimage to Moclín, in the province of Granada, but Lorca convinces us easily of their wholly pagan character. The girls spinning wool in *Blood Wedding* can be justified realistically, but they are also meant to remind us of the Parcae.

There is still another way, beyond the ones already mentioned, in which Lorca's dramas are grounded in mystery: the motivation of his characters. Critics have often tried to reduce these plays to antithetical formulas, or study them as variations on a single theme. All three plays appear to represent a struggle between freedom and repression or a conflict between the individual and society or natural law and social law. If Yerma cannot bear a child, it is, some argue, because a rigid code of societal honor prevents her from abandoning Juan or taking advantage of the fertility rites described in Act III. More or less the same struggle is played out in *Blood Wedding*: the Bride succumbs to her passion, evading what is socially acceptable (marriage with the Bridegroom), and this leads to death. Bernarda's obsession with "what the neighbors will say" contributes, without a doubt, to the suicide of Adela. In all three dramas, characters focus obsessively on a single object—Yerma yearns for a child; the Bride longs for Leonardo; Adela, for Pepe el Romano. And in all three plays desire is frustrated violently and fatally by social forces. Authority appears to triumph over freedom, society over personal instinct, the social law over deeper laws of nature. This message seems especially apt from a playwright whose own sexuality caused him much suffering and whose life was cut short by the advent of political repression. *The House of Bernarda Alba* has often been read as a premonition of the Franco regime, and hearing Bernarda's pathetic final words—"Silence! Silence, I said! Silence!"—one cannot help but remember the censorship that would descend upon Spanish liberal thought, and upon Lorca's own work, for several decades (the play was long banned in Spain).

The social interpretation of these plays is certainly justifiable. Lorca himself encouraged it, both from within the plays and in public statements like those already mentioned. *The House of Bernarda Alba* roundly condemns authoritarianism and the class system which perpetuates it. "The poor are like animals," Bernarda remarks. "They seem to be made of other substances." And, yet the social reading is grossly inadequate. There *is* a fundamental antithesis in Lorca's work, but it is even more inclusive than the struggle between the individual and society.

From his earliest works, Lorca is an elegist, and the social implications of these three plays are but one manifestation of the duality involved in all elegy. Broadly considered, elegy compares two modes of being: presence and absence, what is and what was; how things are and how they might have been. The central theme of all of Lorca's work is indeed desire; as Robert Bly once noted, all of his characters *want* something. But the object of desire is invisible, shadowy, like Pepe el Romano. The plays suggest, not merely that society frustrates our intimate desires and instincts, but that those desires and instincts can never be clearly identified. Lorca's characters are unhappy and tragic, not because society keeps them from attaining their object or reaching their destination, but because they cannot fully understand what it is that they want.

The same dilemma is apparent everywhere in Lorca's poetry, and in his very conception of life. In his meditation upon the *pena negra* (literally, "black sorrow" or "black pain") that is mentioned in the lyrics of Andalusian folk music Lorca had insisted that such pain has no apparent cause. It is, simply, "incurable pain, the black pain we cannot get rid of except by taking a knife and opening a deep buttonhole in our left side." What Lorca says of Soledad Montoya, the gypsy protagonist of one of his *Ballads*, seems applicable also to the characters in his plays:

The pain of Soledad Montoya is the root of the Andalusian people. It is not anguish, because in this pain one can smile, nor does it blind, for it never produces weeping. It is a longing without object, a keen love of nothing, with the certainty that death (the eternal care of Andalusia) is breathing behind the door.

Many of Lorca's most memorable poems give expression to this blind longing: e.g., the "Qasida of the Rose," from his last great elegiac book, *The Divan at Tamarit*:

> *The rose*
> *was not searching for the dawn.*
> *Almost eternal on its stem,*
> *it was seeking something else.*

The rose
was not searching for knowledge or shadow.
Enclosure of flesh and dream,
it was seeking something else.

The rose
was not seeking the rose.
Immobile in the sky,
it was seeking something else!

That "something else" lies beyond language. Poetry and drama are unable to name it, only to gesture toward it. They *are* the gesture: a mysterious stylized gesture toward meaning.

The signs of this indeterminacy are found in all three of the plays, but are most apparent in *Yerma*. What is it that Yerma longs for? Her longing for a child is, somehow, more than that. It is an almost metaphysical search for completion, for the meaning of her own life. When Juan, her husband, tells her to stop fretting and resign herself to her barrenness, he calls attention not only to his own insensitivity but to the indeterminacy of his wife's desire:

I can no longer put up with this constant grieving over obscure things, unreal things made of thin air . . . Over things that have not happened and that neither you nor I can control.

By the final act of the play, Yerma's longing for a child has given way to something much more difficult to define. It is the "keen love of nothing," the uncentered desire of Soledad Montoya. Offered the chance to leave Juan and move in with someone who can give her a child, Yerma protests: "I'm like a parched field big enough to hold a thousand teams of oxen plowing, and what you give me is a little glass of water from the well! Mine is pain that is no longer of my flesh!" The ultimate antithesis, then, is not that of society and the individual but that of presence (the realm of reality) and absence (the realm of the imagination). Yerma's tragedy is not that society keeps her from fulfilling a biological urge or realizing herself fully. It is that she can desire, can imagine and feel an absence, while her husband cannot. "All I care about is what I can hold in my hands," Juan says. "What I can see with my eyes!" Beyond its appeal for justice, for freedom, and for sexual equality, Lorca's theater is a passionate defense of poetry and of the imagination. His characters' search for meaning parallels that of the reader. The result is dramatic poetry, or poetic drama, unsurpassed by any writer of our time.

Christopher Maurer
Vanderbilt University

BLOOD
WEDDING

A TRAGEDY IN THREE ACTS

AND SEVEN SCENES

Cast of Characters

THE BRIDEGROOM

THE BRIDEGROOM'S MOTHER

THE BRIDE

THE BRIDE'S FATHER

LEONARDO

LEONARDO'S WIFE

LEONARDO'S MOTHER-IN-LAW

THE MAID

THE NEIGHBOR

THE MOON

DEATH

THREE WOODCUTTERS

TWO YOUNG MEN

GIRL

THREE GIRLS

LITTLE GIRL

THREE GUESTS

A WOMAN

NEIGHBORS

ACT I

SCENE I

(The room is painted yellow)

BRIDEGROOM

(Entering) Mother?

MOTHER

Yes?

BRIDEGROOM

I'm going.

MOTHER

Where?

BRIDEGROOM

To the vineyard. *(He starts to go)*

MOTHER

Wait.

BRIDEGROOM

Do you need something?

MOTHER

Son, your breakfast!

BRIDEGROOM

Never mind. I'll eat some grapes. Give me the knife.

MOTHER

What for?

BRIDEGROOM

(Laughing) To cut them with.

MOTHER

(Muttering as she looks for it) The knife! The knife! Damn all of them! And the monster who invented them!

BRIDEGROOM

Let's change the subject.

MOTHER

And the shotguns and the pistols and the smallest knife—and even the pitchfork and the hoe!

BRIDEGROOM

Enough!

MOTHER

Anything that can cut into a man's body! A beautiful man, with life like a flower in his mouth, who goes out to the vineyards or to his own olive groves, because they are his, inherited . . .

BRIDEGROOM

(Lowering his head) Mother, be quiet!

MOTHER

. . . and that man does not return. Or if he does, it's only to have a palm placed over him or a dish of rock salt, so his body won't float. I don't know how you dare to carry a knife on you! Or why I allow this serpent inside the cupboard!

BRIDEGROOM

Haven't you said enough?

MOTHER

If I lived a hundred years, I would talk of nothing else! First, your father. To me he smelled like carnations, and I enjoyed him only three short years. Then your brother. Is it fair? How can it be that something as small as a pistol or a knife can destroy a man who is like a bull? I'll never be quiet. The months go by, and the desperation stings my eyes and the very tips of my hair!

BRIDEGROOM

(Loudly) Can't we be done with it?

MOTHER

No, we can't be done with it! Can anyone bring me back your father? Or your brother? And then there is prison. What is a prison? People eat there, they smoke there, they play their music there. My dead ones, covered with weeds, silent, turned to dust. Two men who were like two geraniums! The killers, in prison, alive and well, gazing at the mountains.

BRIDEGROOM

Do you want me to kill them?

MOTHER

No . . . If I talk about it, it's because— How can I *not* talk about it, watching you go out that door? I don't want you to carry a knife. I just . . . I just wish you wouldn't go out to the fields.

BRIDEGROOM

(Laughing) Mother!

MOTHER

How I wish you had been a girl! You wouldn't be going down to the stream now. And we would be embroidering linens and little wool dogs.

BRIDEGROOM

(Takes her by the arm and laughs) Mother, what if I took you with me to the vineyard?

MOTHER

What would an old woman do in the vineyard! Would you hide me under the vine leaves?

BRIDEGROOM

(Lifting her up in his arms) Old woman! Old, old woman! Old, old, old woman!

MOTHER

Your father did take me. That's good stock, good blood! Your grandfather left a son on every corner. That I like—men that are men, wheat that is wheat.

START

BRIDEGROOM

And me, Mother?

MOTHER

What about you?

BRIDEGROOM

Do I have to tell you again?

MOTHER

(Serious) Oh!

BRIDEGROOM

Does it bother you?

MOTHER

No.

BRIDEGROOM

What is it?

MOTHER

I don't know myself. All of a sudden, like this, it always surprises me. I know she's a good girl. That's true, isn't it? Quiet, hard-working. She bakes her bread and sews her skirts—and yet, every time I mention her, I feel as if I'd been struck on the forehead with a rock.

BRIDEGROOM

That's nonsense!

MOTHER

It's not nonsense. I'll be left alone! You're all I have now, and it makes me sad that you'll be leaving.

BRIDEGROOM

But you'll come with us.

MOTHER

No. I can't leave your father and your brother alone here. I have to go to them every morning. And if I go away, one of the Felixes might easily die. One of that family of killers! And they might bury him right next to them. And that—never! Never! Because I will dig him up with my fingernails! And all by myself, I will smash him against the wall!

BRIDEGROOM

(Loudly) Back to that again!

MOTHER

Forgive me.

(Pause)

How long have you been seeing her?

BRIDEGROOM

Three years. I was finally able to buy the vineyard.

MOTHER

Three years. She used to see someone else, didn't she?

BRIDEGROOM

I don't know—I don't think so. Girls have to look carefully at who they are going to marry.

MOTHER

Yes. I didn't look at anyone. I looked at your father, and when they killed him, I looked at the wall in front of me. One woman with one man, and that's it.

BRIDEGROOM

You know my fiancée's a good girl.

MOTHER

I don't doubt it. Anyway, I'm sorry I don't know what her mother was like.

BRIDEGROOM

What does it matter?

MOTHER

(Looking at him) Son!

BRIDEGROOM

What do you want?

MOTHER

It's true! You're right! When do you want me to ask for her?

BRIDEGROOM

(Happily) Would Sunday be all right?

MOTHER

(Seriously) I'll take her those bronze earrings, they're very old. And you buy her—

BRIDEGROOM

You know more—

MOTHER

—buy her some lace stockings. And for yourself, two suits. No, three! You're all I have, now.

BRIDEGROOM

I'm leaving. Tomorrow, I'll go see her.

MOTHER

Yes. Yes. And let's see if you can make me happy with six grandchildren—or as many as you feel like—since your father had no chance to give me any more children of my own.

BRIDEGROOM

The first boy will be for you.

MOTHER

Yes. But have some girls! I want to embroider, and make lace, and be at peace.

BRIDEGROOM

I'm sure you will love her.

MOTHER

I will love her. *(She starts to kiss him, but draws back)* Go on. You're too old for kisses. Give them to your wife. *(She pauses. Then, to herself)* When she *is* your wife!

BRIDEGROOM

I'm leaving.

MOTHER

You better hoe the vines over by the little mill. You've been neglecting them.

BRIDEGROOM

Whatever you say.

MOTHER

God go with you.

(The BRIDEGROOM exits. The MOTHER remains seated, with her back to the door. A NEIGHBOR wearing a dark dress and a scarf on her head appears at the door)

MOTHER

Come in.

NEIGHBOR

How are you?

MOTHER

Same as always.

NEIGHBOR

I came down to the store and dropped in to see you. We live so far apart!

MOTHER

It's been twenty years since I've been up to the top of the road.

NEIGHBOR

You seem well.

MOTHER

You think so?

NEIGHBOR

Things happen. Two days ago they brought in my neighbor's son—with both arms cut off by the machine. *(She sits down)*

MOTHER

Rafael?

NEIGHBOR

Yes. And there you have him. Many times I think your son and mine are better off where they are, asleep, resting, and not in danger of being left useless.

MOTHER

Don't say that. That's all just talk, but it's no consolation.

NEIGHBOR

(She sighs)

MOTHER

(She sighs)

(There is a moment of silence)

NEIGHBOR

(Sadly) Where is your son?

MOTHER

He went out.

NEIGHBOR

He finally bought the vineyard!

MOTHER

He was fortunate.

NEIGHBOR

And now he'll get married.

MOTHER

(As if suddenly roused, she draws her chair nearer to that of her neighbor)
Listen!

NEIGHBOR

(Eager for a confidence) Yes?

MOTHER

Do you know this girl my son wants to marry?

NEIGHBOR

A good girl!

MOTHER

Yes, but . . .

NEIGHBOR

But there is no one who *really* knows her. She lives there alone
with her father, so far away—fifteen miles from the nearest
house. But she's a good girl, accustomed to being alone.

MOTHER

What about her mother?

NEIGHBOR

Her mother, I *did* know— She was beautiful! Her face shone
like a saint's. But I never liked her. She didn't love her husband.

MOTHER

(Harshly) The things some people seem to know!

NEIGHBOR

Pardon me! I didn't mean to offend you, but it's true. Now,
whether or not she was a decent woman, no one said. There's
been no talk about that. She acted so superior.

MOTHER

Always the same!

NEIGHBOR

You asked me.

MOTHER

I just wish that no one knew either the one who's alive or the
one who's dead. I wish they were like two thistles that would
prick any wagging tongue that touched them.

NEIGHBOR

You're right. Your son deserves the best.

MOTHER

The best. That's why I take such care of him . . . I was told the
girl was engaged to another man, some time ago.

NEIGHBOR

She must have been fifteen years old. He got married two years
ago—to one of her cousins, as a matter of fact. No one remembers that engagement.

MOTHER

How is it *you* remember?

NEIGHBOR

You ask me such questions!

MOTHER

We all like to know more about anything that can hurt us. Who
was he?

NEIGHBOR

Leonardo.

MOTHER

Leonardo who?

NEIGHBOR

Leonardo Felix.

MOTHER

(Getting up) Felix!

NEIGHBOR

How could it be Leonardo's fault? He was eight years old when
it happened.

MOTHER

That's true. But I just hear—"Felix!" *(under her breath)*—and hearing "Felix" is like having my mouth fill up with slime! *(She spits)* And I have to spit! I have to spit, so I won't kill!

NEIGHBOR

Control yourself! What do you gain from this?

MOTHER

Nothing. But you do understand.

NEIGHBOR

Don't stand in the way of your son's happiness. Don't say anything to him. You're getting old. So am I. For you and me, it is time to be silent.

MOTHER

I won't say anything to him.

NEIGHBOR

(Kissing her) Nothing.

MOTHER

(Calmly) Such things . . .

NEIGHBOR

I'm leaving. My people will be coming in from the fields soon.

MOTHER

Have you ever seen such a hot day?

NEIGHBOR

The children who take water out to the reapers are black from the sun. Goodbye, my friend.

MOTHER

Goodbye.

(The MOTHER *starts toward the door at the left. Halfway there, she stops and blesses herself)*

CURTAIN

SCENE 2

(The room is painted pink, decorated with copper objects and bunches of everyday flowers. At center, a table with a tablecloth. It is morning. LEONARDO'S MOTHER-IN-LAW *holds a* CHILD *in her arms. She rocks him. The* WIFE *sits in a corner, knitting)*

MOTHER-IN-LAW
Sleep, my child, and dream
About the giant horse
Who didn't want the water.
The water, deep and black,
In among the branches.
Arriving at the bridge,
The water stops and sings.
Who can say, my child,
What the water holds?
—With its flowing tail,
Along its verdant hall.

WIFE
(Softly)
Go to sleep, my flower—
The horse does not want water.

MOTHER-IN-LAW
Go to sleep, my rose—
The horse begins to cry.
His wounded hooves,
His frozen mane,
And in his eyes

A silver dagger.
They went to the river,
Down to the river!
The blood was flowing
Stronger than water.

WIFE

Go to sleep, my flower—
The horse does not want water.

MOTHER-IN-LAW

Go to sleep, my rose—
The horse begins to cry.

WIFE

He would not touch
The riverside.
His mouth was hot
With silver flies.
He only cried
To the hard hills,
With the dead river
Upon his throat.
The giant horse
Did not want water!
Oh, sorrow of snow,
The horse of dawn!

MOTHER-IN-LAW

Stay back! Don't come!
Close the window
With branches of dreams
And dreams of branches.

WIFE

My child is sleeping.

MOTHER-IN-LAW

My child is quiet.

WIFE

O horse, my child
A pillow has.

MOTHER-IN-LAW

His cradle of steel.

WIFE

His blanket of linen.

MOTHER-IN-LAW

Sleep, my child, and dream.

WIFE

Oh, the giant horse
Who did not want the water!

MOTHER-IN-LAW

Don't come! Don't enter!
Go off to the mountain
Through the gray valleys,
The mare awaits.

WIFE
(Looking)

My child is sleeping.

MOTHER-IN-LAW

My child is resting.

WIFE
(Softly)

Go to sleep, my flower—
The horse does not want water.

MOTHER-IN-LAW
(Rising. Very softly)
Go to sleep, my rose—
The horse begins to cry.

(MOTHER-IN-LAW *exits with* CHILD. LEONARDO *enters*)

START

LEONARDO
How's the child?

WIFE
He's sleeping.

LEONARDO
He wasn't well yesterday. He cried during the night.

WIFE
(Happy) Today he's like a dahlia. What about you? Have you been to the blacksmith?

LEONARDO
I just came from there. Would you believe it? For more than two months, I've been putting new shoes on that horse, and they keep coming off. He must be tearing them off on the rocks.

WIFE
Could it be you ride him too much?

LEONARDO
No. I hardly use him at all.

WIFE
Yesterday, the neighbors told me they had seen you at the far end of the drylands.

LEONARDO
Who said that?

WIFE

The women who were out gathering capers. It certainly surprised me. Was it you?

LEONARDO

No. What would I be doing out there in that wasteland?

WIFE

That's what I said. But the horse was drowning in sweat.

LEONARDO

Did you see it?

WIFE

No. My mother did.

LEONARDO

Is she with the child?

WIFE

Yes. Would you like some lemonade?

LEONARDO

With very cold water.

WIFE

Why didn't you come home to eat?

LEONARDO

I was with the wheat buyers. They always keep you.

WIFE

(Making his drink. She speaks tenderly) Are they paying a good price?

LEONARDO

A fair one.

WIFE

I need a dress, and the baby needs a bonnet with bows.

LEONARDO

I'm going in to see him. *(He gets up)*

WIFE

Be careful—he's asleep.

MOTHER-IN-LAW

(As she enters) Who is riding that horse so hard? He's stretched out down there, with his eyes rolling around, as if he'd come from the ends of the earth.

LEONARDO

(Acidly) Me.

MOTHER-IN-LAW

Pardon me! He *is* yours!

WIFE

(Timidly) He was with the wheat buyers.

MOTHER-IN-LAW

Let him die, for all I care! *(She sits down)*

(There is a pause)

WIFE

Your lemonade—is it cold?

LEONARDO

Yes.

WIFE

Did you know they are asking for my cousin's hand?

LEONARDO

When?

WIFE

Tomorrow. The wedding will be within the month. I suppose
they will be coming to invite us.

LEONARDO

(Somberly) I don't know.

MOTHER-IN-LAW

I don't think his mother was very happy about the marriage.

LEONARDO

And perhaps she is right. You have to watch out for her.

WIFE

I don't like you to think badly of a nice girl.

MOTHER-IN-LAW

But he says that because he knows her. Don't you realize they
were seeing each other for three years?

LEONARDO

But I stopped seeing her! *(To his* WIFE*)* Are you going to cry
now? Stop it! *(He brusquely pulls her hands away from her face)*
Let's go see the child.

(They exit, arms around each other. A GIRL *runs in, joyously)*

GIRL

Señora!

MOTHER-IN-LAW

What is it?

GIRL

The bridegroom came to the store, and he's bought the best of everything!

MOTHER-IN-LAW

Did he come by himself?

GIRL

No, with his mother—tall, dignified. *(She imitates her)* And what finery!

MOTHER-IN-LAW

They have money.

GIRL

And they bought some lace stockings. Oh, what stockings! Women dream of such stockings! Look: a swallow here *(she points to her ankle)*, a boat here *(she points to her calf)*, and here *(she points to her thigh)* a rose!

MOTHER-IN-LAW

Child!

GIRL

A rose with the seeds and the stem! Oh, and all done in silk!

MOTHER-IN-LAW

Two wealthy families are going to be joined.

(LEONARDO and his WIFE enter)

GIRL

I came to tell you what they're buying.

LEONARDO

(Harshly) We don't care!

WIFE

Leave her alone.

MOTHER-IN-LAW

Leonardo, don't make so much of it!

GIRL

Please excuse me. *(She leaves, weeping)*

MOTHER-IN-LAW

Why do you always have to pick on people?

LEONARDO

I didn't ask for your opinion. *(He sits down)*

MOTHER-IN-LAW

Very well!

(Pause)

WIFE

What is wrong with you? What scheme is boiling up inside your
head? Don't leave me this way—not knowing anything—

LEONARDO

Get away!

WIFE

No. I want you to look at me and tell me.

LEONARDO

Leave me alone. *(He gets up)*

WIFE

Where are you going?

LEONARDO

(Bitterly) Will you be quiet?

MOTHER-IN-LAW

(Resolutely, to her daughter) Sssh!

*(*LEONARDO *exits)*

The child! *(She exits, and comes back with the child in her arms)*

(The WIFE *remains standing, motionless)*

His wounded hooves,
His frozen mane,
And in his eyes
A silver dagger.

They went to the river,
Down to the river!
The blood was flowing
Stronger than water.

WIFE

(Turning slowly, as if in a dream)
Go to sleep, my flower,
The horse begins to drink.

MOTHER-IN-LAW

Go to sleep, my rose,
The horse begins to cry.

WIFE

Sleep, my child, and dream.

MOTHER-IN-LAW

Oh, the giant horse
Who did not want the water!

WIFE

(Dramatically)
Don't come! Don't enter!

Go off to the mountain.
Oh, sorrow of snow,
The horse of dawn.

MOTHER-IN-LAW
(Weeping)
My child is sleeping.

WIFE
(Weeping as she slowly moves closer)
My child is resting.

MOTHER-IN-LAW
Go to sleep, my flower,
The horse begins to drink.

WIFE
(Weeping, supporting herself on the table)
Go to sleep, my rose,
The horse begins to cry.

CURTAIN

SCENE 3

(Interior of the cave where the BRIDE *lives. Upstage, a cross of large pink flowers. The archway doors have lace curtains tied with pink bows. On the hard white masonry walls are round open fans, blue vases, and small mirrors. The* MAID *is onstage. The* BRIDEGROOM *and his* MOTHER *enter. The* MOTHER *is dressed in black satin and wears a lace mantilla. The* BRIDEGROOM *wears a black corduroy suit and a large gold chain)*

MAID
(Affably, full of hypocritical humility) Come in. Would you like to sit down? They'll be right here. *(She exits)*

(Mother and son remain seated, as immobile as statues. A long pause)

MOTHER

Did you bring the watch?

BRIDEGROOM

Yes. *(He takes it out and looks at it)*

MOTHER

We have to get back in time. How far away these people live!

BRIDEGROOM

But the land here is good.

MOTHER

Good, but much too lonely. Four hours on the road, and not a house or a tree!

BRIDEGROOM

These are the drylands.

MOTHER

Your father would have covered them with trees.

BRIDEGROOM

Without water?

MOTHER

He would have found it. The three years he was married to me, he planted ten cherry trees— *(She thinks back)* The three walnuts by the mill, one whole vineyard and a plant called Jupiter, with blood-red flowers, but it died.

(Pause)

BRIDEGROOM

She must be getting dressed.

(The BRIDE's FATHER *enters—an elderly man with shining white hair. His head is inclined. The* MOTHER *and the* BRIDEGROOM *stand to shake hands silently)*

FATHER

Was it a long journey?

MOTHER

Four hours.

(They sit down)

FATHER

You must have come the long way.

MOTHER

I am too old now to walk along the cliffs by the river.

BRIDEGROOM

She gets dizzy.

(Pause)

FATHER

A good hemp harvest.

BRIDEGROOM

Truly good.

FATHER

In my time, not even hemp would grow on this land. You had to punish it, even cry over it, before it would provide us with something.

MOTHER

But now it does. Don't complain—I didn't come to ask you for anything.

FATHER

(Smiling) You are richer than I am. Your vineyards are worth a fortune. Each young vine a silver coin! I'm only sorry that our lands—you understand?—are separated. I like everything together. There's one thorn in my heart, and it's that little orchard stuck right in the middle of my property. They won't sell it to me for all the gold in the world.

BRIDEGROOM

It's always that way.

FATHER

If we could take twenty teams of oxen and bring your vineyards over here and put them on the hillside— What joy!

MOTHER

What for?

FATHER

What's mine is hers, and what's yours is his, that's why! To see it all together. Because together is beautiful.

BRIDEGROOM

And it would be less work.

MOTHER

When I die, you can sell that place and buy next to this one.

FATHER

Sell? Sell! Bah! Buy, my dear, buy it all! If I had sons, I would have bought this whole hill, as far as the stream. It's not good land, but with muscle you make it good. And since people don't come this way, they don't steal your crops, and you can sleep peacefully.

MOTHER

(After a pause) You know why I've come.

FATHER

Yes.

MOTHER

Well?

FATHER

I think it's fine. They have talked it over.

MOTHER

My son has what it takes.

FATHER

My daughter, too.

MOTHER

My son is a good man. He has never known a woman. His reputation is cleaner than a sheet spread out in the sun.

FATHER

What can I tell you about my daughter? She makes bread at three, while the morning star is still shining. She never talks— soft as wool. She embroiders all kinds of embroidery. And she can cut through a rope with her teeth.

MOTHER

God bless your house!

FATHER

May God bless it.

(The MAID enters with two trays—one with wineglasses, the other with sweets)

MOTHER

(To BRIDEGROOM) When do you want the wedding?

BRIDEGROOM

Next Thursday.

FATHER

The day on which she will be exactly twenty-two years old.

MOTHER

Twenty-two years old. That would be the age of my eldest son, if he were alive. And how alive he'd be—warm and manly as he was!—if men hadn't invented knives!

FATHER

One shouldn't think about that.

MOTHER

Every minute. Look into your own heart.

FATHER

Thursday, then. Isn't that right?

BRIDEGROOM

That's right.

FATHER

The bride and groom and the two of us will go to church in the carriage, since it's so far. And the wedding party in their own carts and on their own horses.

MOTHER

Agreed.

(The MAID *crosses the stage)*

FATHER

Tell her that she can come in now. *(To the* MOTHER*)* I'll be very pleased if you like her.

(The BRIDE *enters, her hands modestly at her sides, her head lowered)*

MOTHER

Come closer. Are you happy?

BRIDE

Yes, *señora*.

FATHER

You shouldn't look so serious. When all is said and done, she's going to be your mother!

BRIDE

I am happy. When I said yes, it was because I wanted to.

MOTHER

Of course. *(Taking her by the chin)* Look at me.

FATHER

She's like my wife, in every way.

MOTHER

Yes? What beautiful eyes! Do you know what being married is, child?

BRIDE

(Gravely) I know.

MOTHER

One man, some children—and a wall six feet thick, to shut out everything else.

BRIDEGROOM

Is anything else needed?

MOTHER

No . . . Just that you all live. Just that! Live!

BRIDE

I will know my duty.

MOTHER

Here are some presents.

BRIDE

Thank you.

FATHER

Shall we have something?

MOTHER

Nothing for me. *(To the* BRIDEGROOM*)* What about you?

BRIDEGROOM

I will.

(He takes a sweet. The BRIDE *takes one also)*

FATHER

(To the BRIDEGROOM*)* Some wine?

MOTHER

He doesn't touch it.

FATHER

That is best.

(Pause. Everyone is standing)

BRIDEGROOM

(To the BRIDE*)* I'll come tomorrow.

BRIDE

At what time?

BRIDEGROOM

At five.

BRIDE

I'll be waiting for you.

BRIDEGROOM

When I leave your side, I feel so lost, and I get a lump in my throat.

BRIDE

When you're my husband, you won't feel that way.

BRIDEGROOM

That's what I say.

MOTHER

We must go. The sun does not wait. *(To the* FATHER*)* Is everything agreed?

FATHER

Agreed.

MOTHER

(To the MAID*)* Goodbye.

MAID

Go with God.

(The MOTHER *kisses the* BRIDE, *and they start to leave in silence)*

MOTHER

(At the door) Goodbye, daughter.

(The BRIDE *answers with her hand)*

FATHER

I will go out with you.

(They leave)

MAID

I'm bursting to see the presents!

BRIDE

(Harshly) Get away!

MAID

Oh, child, show them to me!

BRIDE

I don't want to.

MAID

At least the stockings! They say they're all lace! Please!

BRIDE

I said no!

MAID

For heaven's sake! All right. You're acting like you don't want to get married.

BRIDE

(Biting her hand in rage) Oh!

MAID

Child! My dear! What's the matter with you? Are you sorry you're giving up the life of a queen? Don't think about unpleasant things! Is there any reason? None. Let's look at the presents. *(She takes the box)*

BRIDE

(Seizing her by the wrists) Let go!

MAID

Oh, child!

BRIDE

Let go, I said!

MAID

You're stronger than a man!

BRIDE

Haven't I done the work of a man? If only I *were* a man!

MAID

Don't talk like that!

BRIDE

Be quiet, I said! Let's talk about something else.

(*The light begins to fade. A long pause*)

MAID

Did you hear a horse last night?

BRIDE

At what time?

MAID

At three o'clock.

BRIDE

It must have been a horse that strayed from the herd.

MAID

No, it had a rider.

BRIDE

How do you know that?

MAID

Because I saw him. He was standing under your window. It really surprised me.

BRIDE

Could it have been my fiancé? Sometimes he comes by at that
hour.

MAID

No.

BRIDE

Did you see him?

MAID

Yes.

BRIDE

Who was it?

MAID

It was Leonardo.

BRIDE

(Loud) That's a lie! A lie! What would he come here for?

MAID

He came.

BRIDE

Shut up! Damn your tongue!

(The sound of hoofbeats is heard)

MAID

(At the window) Look—out there! Was it him?

BRIDE

It was him.

FAST CURTAIN

ACT II

SCENE I

(The veranda of the BRIDE's *house. The front door is upstage. It is night. The* BRIDE *comes out, dressed in ruffled white petticoats covered with lace and embroidered scallops, a white bodice, her arms bare. The* MAID *is dressed as before)*

MAID

I'll finish combing your hair out here.

BRIDE

It's impossible to stay indoors in this heat!

MAID

It never cools off around here, not even at dawn!

(The BRIDE *sits down in a low chair and looks at herself in a small hand mirror. The* MAID *combs her hair)*

BRIDE

My mother came from a place where there were many trees, from a fertile land.

MAID

That's why she was so cheerful.

BRIDE

But she wasted away here.

MAID

Fate.

BRIDE

Just as we women all waste away. The walls are throwing off heat! Ouch! Don't pull so much!

MAID

I just want to do this wave better. I want it to fall over your forehead.

(The BRIDE *looks at herself in the mirror)*

How beautiful you are! Oh! *(She kisses her with great affection)*

BRIDE

(Severely) Keep combing my hair.

MAID

(Combing) You are so lucky! You're going to hold a man in your arms. You're going to kiss him. You're going to feel his weight!

BRIDE

Be quiet!

MAID

And the best part is when you wake up and you feel him beside you and his breath caresses your shoulder, like a nightingale's feather!

BRIDE

(Fiercely) Will you be quiet!

MAID

But, child! A wedding—what is it? A wedding is that, and nothing more! Is it the wedding cake? Is it the bouquets of flowers? No! It's a shining bed, and a man, and a woman!

BRIDE

You're not supposed to talk about it!

MAID

That's something else. But it's such fun!

BRIDE

Or such misery!

MAID

I am going to set the orange blossoms from here to here, so they form a crown on your hair. *(She tries on the orange blossoms)*

BRIDE

(Looking in the mirror) Give it to me. *(She takes the orange blossoms, looks at them, and hangs her head dejectedly)*

MAID

What is this?

BRIDE

Leave me alone.

MAID

This is no time to be sad. *(With spirit)* Give me those flowers!

(The BRIDE *throws down the flowers)*

Child, you're asking for trouble, throwing your crown on the floor! Lift up that head. Don't you want to get married? Say so. You can still change your mind.

(The BRIDE *stands up)*

BRIDE

They are dark clouds—an ill wind inside me. Who hasn't felt that?

MAID

Do you love him?

BRIDE

I love him.

MAID

Yes, yes. I'm sure.

BRIDE

But this is a very big step.

MAID

You have to take it.

BRIDE

I have already given my promise.

MAID

I am going to put the crown on you.

BRIDE

(Sitting down) Hurry! They should be arriving soon.

MAID

They've been on the road at least two hours.

BRIDE

How far is it from here to the church?

MAID

Five leagues by way of the stream, but it's twice as far along the road.

(The BRIDE stands; the MAID gazes at her with excitement)

> The bride is awakening
> On the morning of the wedding!
> The rivers of the world
> Carry your crown!

BRIDE

(Smiling) Come on!

MAID

(Kisses BRIDE *and dances around her)*

> Let her awaken
> With the tender blossom
> Of the laurel in flower!
>
> May she awaken
> By the trunk and the branch
> Of the laurel in flower!

(There is a loud knocking)

BRIDE

Open it! It must be the first guests!

(The BRIDE *goes into the house. The* MAID *opens the door)*

MAID

(Surprised) You?

LEONARDO

Me. Good morning.

MAID

You're the first one.

LEONARDO

Wasn't I invited?

MAID

Yes.

LEONARDO

That's why I came.

MAID

Where's your wife?

LEONARDO

I rode the horse. She's coming along the road.

MAID

Didn't you come across anyone?

LEONARDO

I passed them on my horse.

MAID

You're going to kill that animal with so much hard riding!

LEONARDO

When he dies, he's dead.

(Pause)

MAID

Sit down. Nobody's up yet.

LEONARDO

What about the bride?

MAID

I am going to dress her right now.

LEONARDO

The *bride*! She must be happy.

MAID

(Changing the subject) Where is the child?

LEONARDO

What child?

Your son.

LEONARDO

(As if from a daze) Oh.

MAID

Are they bringing him?

LEONARDO

No.

(Pause. In the distance, voices are singing)

VOICES

The bride is awakening
On the morning of the wedding!

LEONARDO

The bride is awakening
On the morning of the wedding!

MAID

It's the people. They are still a way off.

LEONARDO

(Rising) The bride will wear a large crown, won't she? It shouldn't be too large. A smaller one would suit her better. Did the groom bring the orange blossom she's to wear on her breast?

(The BRIDE enters, still in petticoats, wearing the crown of blossoms)

BRIDE

He brought it.

MAID

Don't come out here like that!

BRIDE

What does it matter? *(Coldly)* Why do you ask if they brought the orange blossom? Do you have something in mind?

LEONARDO

Nothing. What would I have in mind? *(Approaching her)* You know me—you know I don't. Tell me, what have I ever been to you? Look back and refresh your memory! Two oxen and a tumbledown hut are almost nothing. That's what hurts.

BRIDE

Why did you come?

LEONARDO

To see your wedding.

BRIDE

Just as I saw yours!

LEONARDO

You tied the knot with your own two hands. They can kill me, but they can't spit on me! And gold may glisten—but sometimes it spits!

BRIDE

That's a lie!

LEONARDO

I don't want to talk about it, because I'm hot-blooded, and I don't want all these hills to hear my shouts.

BRIDE

My shouts would be louder!

MAID

This conversation cannot continue! You must not talk about the past. *(She glances uneasily at the doors)*

BRIDE

She's right. I shouldn't even be talking to you. But it makes my blood boil to have you come and watch me, and pry into my wedding, and make insinuations about the orange blossom. Get out! And wait for your wife at the door!

LEONARDO

You mean you and I can't talk?

MAID

(Furious) No! You can't talk!

LEONARDO

Since my wedding, I've thought night and day about who was guilty. And every time I think about it, there is a new guilt that swallows up the old. But there is always guilt.

BRIDE

A man on his horse knows a lot, and he has the power to squeeze the life out of a lonely girl stranded in a desert. But I have pride—that's why I'm getting married! And I will shut myself up with my husband, whom I must love more than anything!

LEONARDO

Pride won't do you any good. *(He comes closer)*

BRIDE

Don't come near me!

LEONARDO

To keep still when we're on fire is the worst punishment we can inflict on ourselves. What good did it do me to have pride? —and not see you?—and leave you lying awake, night after night? No good at all! It only poured fire over me! Because you may believe that time can heal and walls can hide—but it's not true. It's not true! When things reach deep inside you, nothing can pull them out!

BRIDE

(Trembling) I can't listen to you! I can't listen to your voice! It's as if I drank a bottle of anisette and fell asleep on a quilt of roses. And it draws me under, and I know I'm drowning, but I follow.

MAID

(Seizing LEONARDO *by the lapels)* You must leave here right now!

LEONARDO

It's the last time I'll ever talk to her. Don't worry about a thing.

BRIDE

And I know I'm crazy, and I know I'm rotting away with the suffering, and here I am—quietly listening to him, watching him move his arms!

LEONARDO

I can't have peace if I don't tell you these things. *I* got married. Now *you* get married!

MAID

She *is* getting married!

VOICES

(Nearer now)
The bride is awakening
On the morning of the wedding!

BRIDE

The bride is awakening! *(She exits, running to her room)*

MAID

The people are here now. *(To* LEONARDO*)* Don't come near her again!

LEONARDO

Don't worry.

(He exits, stage left. It begins to grow lighter)

FIRST GIRL
(Entering)
The bride is awakening
On the morning of the wedding!
The circle turns, and brings a crown
To every balcony.

VOICES
The bride is awakening!

MAID
(Inspiring their cheers)
Let her awaken
With the tender blossom
Of love in flower.

Let her awaken
By the trunk and the branch
Of the laurel in flower.

SECOND GIRL
(Entering)
Let her awaken
With her long hair flowing,
A nightgown of snowflakes,
Silver leather slippers,
And jasmine on her forehead.

MAID
O Shepherdess,
The moon is rising!

FIRST GIRL
O gallant lover,
Leave your hat in the orchard!

FIRST YOUNG MAN
(Enters with his hat held high)
The bride is awakening
The guests are arriving
To dance at her wedding,
With trays of dahlias,
And cakes for the wedding.

MAID
The bride is awakening!

SECOND GIRL
The bride is now wearing
Her white bridal crown.
The bridegroom has pinned it
With ribbons of gold.

MAID
Under the grapefruit tree
The bride is unable to sleep.

THIRD GIRL
(Entering)
Under the orange tree, the groom
Offers a tablecloth, a spoon.

(Three GUESTS enter)

FIRST YOUNG MAN
Awaken, my dove!
The white dawn unburdens
Bells in the shade.

GUEST
The bride, the white bride—
Today a maiden,
Tomorrow a woman.

FIRST GIRL

Come down, dusky maiden,
Trailing your train made of silk.

GUEST

Come down, dusky maiden,
Fresh with the cool morning dew.

FIRST YOUNG MAN

Awaken, *señora*, awaken!
As orange blossoms rain through the air.

MAID

I want to embroider a tree
Covered with garnet ribbons,
With words of love on each ribbon,
And shouts of praise all around!

VOICES

The bride is awakening!

FIRST YOUNG MAN

On the morning of the wedding!

GUEST

On the morning of the wedding,
How enchanting you will be—
Like a flower of the mountains!
Like the wife of a captain!

FATHER
(Entering)

The wife of a captain
Is taking the bridegroom!
He comes with his oxen
To capture the treasure!

The bridegroom is golden—
A golden flower.
Wherever he travels
There are flowers in his footsteps.

MAID

O my happy child!

SECOND YOUNG MAN
(Entering)
The bride is awakening!

MAID

O my enchantress!

FIRST GIRL

The wedding guests are calling
Underneath your window.

SECOND GIRL

The bride will come out now!

FIRST GIRL

Come out now! Come out now!

MAID

They're ringing!
Bells are ringing!

FIRST YOUNG MAN

She's coming here!
She's coming now!

MAID

The wedding looms
Like a bull in the ring!

(The BRIDE appears. She wears a turn-of-the-century black dress, with flowers at the hip, a long train covered with pleated gauze and heavy lace, and the crown of orange blossoms in her hair. Guitars play. The GIRLS kiss the BRIDE)

THIRD GIRL
What perfume did you put in her hair?

BRIDE
(Laughing) None!

SECOND GIRL
(Looking at her dress) You won't find material like this anywhere!

FIRST YOUNG MAN
Here's the groom!

BRIDEGROOM
(Entering) Greetings!

FIRST GIRL
(Putting a flower behind his ear)
The groom is gold—
A golden flower.

SECOND GIRL
A peaceful light
Shines from his eyes.

(The BRIDEGROOM goes to the BRIDE's side)

BRIDE
Why did you wear those shoes?

BRIDEGROOM
They're more cheerful than the black ones.

(LEONARDO'S WIFE enters and kisses the BRIDE)

WIFE

Best wishes!

(The CROWD *is chattering loudly)*

LEONARDO
(Entering as if to fulfill a duty)
On the morning of your marriage
We are crowning you with flowers.

WIFE

So the meadows may be merry
With the fragrance of your hair.

MOTHER
(To FATHER*)* Are those people here, too?

FATHER

They are family. Today is a day for forgiveness.

MOTHER

I put up with them, but I won't forgive them!

BRIDEGROOM

It makes me happy to see you wearing your crown!

BRIDE

Let's leave for the church soon.

BRIDEGROOM

Are you in a hurry?

BRIDE

Yes. I am longing to be your wife. And to be alone with you
and hear no voice but yours.

BRIDEGROOM

That's what I want.

BRIDE

And see no other eyes but yours. And have you hold me so tight
that even if my dead mother called to me I couldn't pull myself
away from you.

BRIDEGROOM

My arms are strong. I am going to hold you for the next forty
years.

BRIDE

(Dramatically, taking him by the arm) Always!

FATHER

Let's go right away! Get the horses and the carts! The sun has
already come up!

MOTHER

But be careful. Let's not have anything go wrong.

(The large door upstage opens, and they begin to exit)

MAID
(Weeping)
On leaving your house,
Maiden so pure,
Remember: you leave
Like a star!

FIRST GIRL
Clear are your body and gown,
Leaving your house for the wedding!

SECOND GIRL
(As they leave)
You're leaving your home
To go to the church.

MAID

The breeze is tossing flowers
Along the sands.

THIRD GIRL

Oh, the girl is pure!

MAID

The lace of her mantilla
Is like a shady breeze.

(They exit. We hear the music of guitars, castanets, and tambourines. LEONARDO *and his* WIFE *are left alone on the stage)*

WIFE

Let's go.

LEONARDO

Where?

WIFE

To the church. But you're not going on your horse, you're coming with me.

LEONARDO

In the cart?

WIFE

What other way?

LEONARDO

I am not a man who rides in a cart!

WIFE

And I am not a woman who goes to a wedding without her husband. I can't stand it anymore!

LEONARDO

Neither can I.

WIFE

Why do you look at me like that? There's a dagger in each eye!

LEONARDO

Let's go!

WIFE

I don't know what's going on. But I imagine things, and I don't want to. One thing I know: I've already been tossed aside! But I have a son. And another on the way. Let's get started. My mother had the same fate. But I'm not leaving here alone!

(VOICES are heard outside)

VOICES
On leaving your house
To go to the church,
Remember: you leave
Like a star!

WIFE
(Weeping)
Remember: you leave
Like a star!

That's how I left my house, too! I could taste the whole world in my mouth!

LEONARDO

(Rising) Let's go!

WIFE

But with me!

Yes.

(Pause)

Get moving!

(They exit)

VOICES
On leaving your house
To go to the church,
Remember: you leave
Like a star!

SLOW CURTAIN

SCENE 2

(The exterior of the BRIDE's cave. Shades of white, grays, and cool blues. Large prickly pears. Somber, silvered tones. Views of tablelands the color of paste, and everything as hard as a landscape on a piece of ceramic folk art. The MAID is arranging glasses and trays on a table)

MAID
Turning—
The wheel was turning,
And the water was flowing.
The wedding approaches!
Let the branches spread open
And the moon embellish
Her white veranda!

(Loudly) Spread the tablecloths!

(With pathos)
Singing—
The lovers were singing,
And the water was flowing.
The wedding approaches!
Let the frost shine and sparkle!
Let the bitter almonds
Be filled with honey!

(Loudly) Bring out the wine!

(Poetically)
My lady—
My lady of the land,
See the water flowing!
Your wedding approaches!
You must gather your trousseau
Under the wing of your bridegroom.
Never go from your house—
Because your bridegroom's a dove,
With his whole heart an ember!

The fields await the murmur
Of the blood that has been spilled.
Turning—
The wheel was turning,
And the water was flowing.
Your wedding approaches!
Let the water be glowing!

MOTHER
(Entering with FATHER*)* At last!

FATHER
Are we the first?

MAID

No. Leonardo arrived with his wife a while ago. They must have driven like demons! His wife arrived frightened to death. They got here as quickly as if they had come on horseback.

FATHER

That man looks for trouble. He has bad blood.

MOTHER

What blood could he have? —That of his whole family, beginning with his great-grandfather who started the killing, and on through the whole evil clan! Men who use knives! People with false smiles!

FATHER

Let's leave it alone!

MAID

How can she leave it alone?

MOTHER

I ache down to the end of my veins! On all their faces, I see nothing but the hand that killed what was mine. Do you see me? Don't I seem mad to you? Well, I am mad—from not having shouted out everything I needed to. I have a scream in my throat—always there—that I have to choke back and hide under my shawl. But they carry off the dead and you must keep silent. Or people will criticize. *(She takes off her shawl)*

FATHER

Today is not the day for you to be remembering those things.

MOTHER

When it comes up in conversation, I have to speak. And today more than ever, because today I'm left alone in my house.

FATHER

In hopes of having new company.

MOTHER

That's my dream. Grandchildren.

(They sit down)

FATHER

I want them to have many. This land needs hands that are not hired. We have to keep up a battle—with weeds, thistles, and rocks that come from who knows where. And these hands should belong to the owners—hands that will punish and will dominate and will sow the seeds. Many sons are needed.

MOTHER

And some daughters! Boys are like the wind. They are forced to use weapons. Girls never leave the house.

FATHER

(Cheerfully) I think they'll have some of everything!

MOTHER

My son will have her pregnant in no time. He comes from good stock. His father could have had many sons with me.

FATHER

What I would like is for it all to happen in one day! For them to have two or three grown sons right away!

MOTHER

But it's not like that. It takes so much time. That's why it's so terrible to see your own blood spilled on the ground. A fountain that flows for a minute—and takes years out of our lives! When I got to see my son, he was lying in the middle of the street. I wet my hands with blood, and I licked them with my tongue. Because it was mine! You don't know what that is! I would place the earth soaked with his blood in an urn of crystal and topaz!

Now you must wait. My daughter is healthy and your son is strong.

MOTHER

I hope so.

(They stand up)

FATHER

Prepare the trays of wheat!

MAID

They are ready.

WIFE

(Entering, with LEONARDO*)* Congratulations!

MOTHER

Thank you.

LEONARDO

Will there be a fiesta?

FATHER

A small one. People can't stay too late.

MAID

They have arrived!

*(*GUESTS *begin entering in lively groups. The* BRIDE *and* BRIDE-GROOM *enter, arm in arm.* LEONARDO *exits)*

BRIDEGROOM

I've never seen so many people at a wedding!

BRIDE

(Gloomily) Never.

FATHER

It was magnificent!

MOTHER

Entire families have come!

BRIDEGROOM

People who never left their houses!

MOTHER

Your father sowed the seed, and now you reap the harvest.

BRIDEGROOM

There were cousins of mine that I didn't know anymore!

MOTHER

All the people from the coast.

BRIDEGROOM

(Laughing) They were frightened by the horses!

(Everyone is talking)

MOTHER

(To the BRIDE*)* What are you thinking about?

BRIDE

I'm not thinking about anything.

MOTHER

The wedding vows weigh heavily.

(Guitars are playing)

BRIDE

Like lead!

MOTHER

(Strongly) But they shouldn't! You should feel as light as a dove.

BRIDE

Are you staying here tonight?

MOTHER

No. There is no one at my house.

BRIDE

You should stay!

FATHER

(To MOTHER*)* Look at the dance they have started! Dances from far away by the edge of the sea.

*(*LEONARDO *enters and sits down. His* WIFE *stands behind him, stiffly)*

MOTHER

(On her way out) They are my husband's cousins. As hard as rocks when they dance.

FATHER

I enjoy watching them. What a change for this house! *(He exits)*

BRIDEGROOM

(To BRIDE*)* Did you like the orange blossoms?

BRIDE

(Staring at him) Yes.

BRIDEGROOM

It's all made of wax. It lasts forever. I would have liked you to wear them all over your dress.

BRIDE

There's no need.

FIRST GIRL

Let's go take off your pins.

BRIDE

(To the BRIDEGROOM*)* I'll be right back.

WIFE

I hope you will be happy with my cousin!

BRIDEGROOM

I'm sure I will be.

WIFE

The two of you here, without ever leaving, raising a family. How I wish I, too, could live this far away!

BRIDEGROOM

Why don't you buy some land? It's cheap on the hillside, and better for raising children.

WIFE

We don't have any money. And the way things are going . . .

BRIDEGROOM

Your husband is a hard worker.

WIFE

Yes. But he likes to move around too much. He goes from one thing to another. He's very restless.

MAID

Aren't you eating anything? I am going to wrap up some wine biscuits for your mother—she likes them so much.

BRIDEGROOM

Give her three dozen.

WIFE

No, no! Half a dozen will be enough.

BRIDEGROOM

This is a special day.

WIFE

(To the MAID*)* Where is Leonardo?

MAID

I didn't see him.

BRIDEGROOM

He must be with the others.

WIFE

I will go and see! *(She leaves)*

MAID

That is beautiful!

BRIDEGROOM

You're not dancing?

MAID

No one asked me.

*(*TWO GIRLS *cross upstage. During this entire scene, people are crossing upstage, animatedly)*

BRIDEGROOM

(Cheerfully) That's because they don't know any better. Lively old ladies like you dance better than young ones.

MAID

Are you trying to flatter me, young man? That family of yours! Men among men! When I was a child, I went to your grandfather's wedding. What a figure he cut! It was as if a mountain was getting married!

                          BRIDEGROOM
I am not as tall.

                          MAID
But you have the same gleam in your eyes. Where's the child?

                          BRIDEGROOM
Taking off her crown.

                          MAID
Ah! Look, for midnight, since you won't be asleep, I put out ham and some large glasses of old wine. In the lower part of the cupboard. In case you need it.

                          BRIDEGROOM
(Smiling) I don't eat at midnight.

                          MAID
If not you, the bride. (She exits)

                          FIRST YOUNG MAN
(Entering) You have to drink with us!

                          BRIDEGROOM
I am waiting for the bride.

                          SECOND YOUNG MAN
Her, you'll have at daybreak!

                          FIRST YOUNG MAN
That's when it's the most fun!

                          SECOND YOUNG MAN
Just for a minute!

BRIDEGROOM

Let's go.

(They exit. There is much chatter. The BRIDE *enters. The* TWO
GIRLS *run to meet her from the opposite side of the stage)*

FIRST GIRL

Who did you give the first pin to, to me or to her?

BRIDE

I don't remember.

FIRST GIRL

You gave it to me, here!

SECOND GIRL

To me, in front of the altar!

BRIDE

(Restless, in a great inner struggle) I don't know anything.

FIRST GIRL

I just wish that you'd—

BRIDE

(Interrupting) And I don't care! I have a lot to think about.

SECOND GIRL

Excuse me.

*(*LEONARDO *crosses upstage)*

BRIDE

(Seeing LEONARDO*)* And these are anxious moments.

FIRST GIRL

We don't know anything!

BRIDE

You will know when your time comes. This step is one that costs you dearly.

FIRST GIRL

Are you upset with us?

BRIDE

No. Please forgive me.

SECOND GIRL

For what? But either pin means you get married, doesn't it?

BRIDE

Both.

FIRST GIRL

But one of us will get married before the other.

BRIDE

Do you want it so badly?

SECOND GIRL

(Shyly) Yes.

BRIDE

Why?

FIRST GIRL

Well . . .

(FIRST GIRL *embraces the other. They both run off. The* BRIDE-GROOM *enters and very slowly embraces the* BRIDE *from behind*)

BRIDE

(Startled) Get away!

BRIDEGROOM

Do I frighten you?

BRIDE

Oh! It was you?

BRIDEGROOM

Who would it be?

(Pause)

Your father or me.

BRIDE

That's true.

BRIDEGROOM

But your father would have embraced you more gently.

BRIDE

(Gloomily) Of course.

(The BRIDEGROOM *hugs her tightly, in a brusque manner)*

BRIDEGROOM

Because he is old!

BRIDE

(Dryly) Let me go.

BRIDEGROOM

Why? *(He lets her go)*

BRIDE

Because . . . people . . . They can see us!

(The MAID *crosses upstage again, without looking at the couple)*

BRIDEGROOM

What of it? It is blessed now!

BRIDE

Yes, but let me go. Later.

BRIDEGROOM

What is wrong? You seem frightened.

BRIDE

Nothing is wrong.

(LEONARDO's WIFE *enters*)

Don't go.

WIFE

I don't want to interrupt . . .

BRIDEGROOM

What is it?

WIFE

Did my husband come through here?

BRIDE

No.

WIFE

You see, I can't find him. And his horse isn't in the stable, either.

BRIDEGROOM

(Cheerfully) He must be out riding.

(*The* WIFE *exits, uneasy. The* MAID *enters*)

MAID

Aren't you happy with so many good wishes?

BRIDEGROOM

I wish it were over already. The bride is a little tired.

MAID

What is it, child?

BRIDE

There's a sort of pounding in my temples.

MAID

In these hills, a bride must be strong. *(To the* BRIDEGROOM*)* You're the only one who can cure her, because she belongs to you. *(The* MAID *goes off quickly)*

BRIDEGROOM

(Embracing her) Let's join the dancing awhile. *(He kisses her)*

BRIDE

(In anguish) No. I want to lie down awhile.

BRIDEGROOM

I'll keep you company.

BRIDE

Never! With all these people here? What would they say? Let me rest a moment.

BRIDEGROOM

Whatever you like. But don't be like this tonight!

BRIDE

(At the door) By tonight I will be better.

BRIDEGROOM

That's what I want.

(The MOTHER *enters)*

MOTHER

Son.

BRIDEGROOM

Where have you been?

MOTHER

In all that noise. Are you happy?

BRIDEGROOM

Yes.

MOTHER

Where is your wife?

BRIDEGROOM

She's resting a little. It's a bad day for brides.

MOTHER

A bad day? It's the only good one! For me, it was like coming into an inheritance!

(The MAID *enters and goes toward the* BRIDE's *room)*

It's the plowing of land, the planting of new trees.

BRIDEGROOM

Are you going to leave?

MOTHER

Yes. I have to be at my house.

BRIDEGROOM

Alone.

MOTHER

Not alone. My head is full of things—and men and struggles.

BRIDEGROOM

But struggles that are no longer struggles.

(The MAID enters quickly. She exits upstage, running)

MOTHER

While you live, you struggle.

BRIDEGROOM

I always respect your wishes.

MOTHER

With your wife, try to be affectionate. And if you notice her being distant or shy, caress her in a way that will hurt her a bit. A tight hug, a little bite—and then a soft kiss. Not enough to upset her, but enough for her to know you are the man, the master, the one who gives the orders. That's how I learned from your father. And since you don't have him, I must be the one to teach you these strategies.

BRIDEGROOM

I will always do what you say.

FATHER

(Entering) Where is my daughter?

BRIDEGROOM

She's inside.

(The FATHER goes inside)

FIRST GIRL

Come on, bride and groom! We're going to dance the Wheel!

FIRST YOUNG MAN
(To BRIDEGROOM*)* You're going to lead it.

FATHER
(As he comes out) She's not here!

BRIDEGROOM
No?

FATHER
She must have gone out on the veranda.

BRIDEGROOM
I'm going to see!

(He exits. Crowd noises and guitars are heard)

FIRST GIRL
They've already started! *(She exits)*

BRIDEGROOM
(Entering) She's not there.

MOTHER
(Uneasy) No?

FATHER
Where could she have gone?

MAID
(Entering) The child, where is she?

MOTHER
(Gravely) We don't know.

(The BRIDEGROOM *exits. Three* GUESTS *enter)*

FATHER

(Dramatically) But isn't she in the dance?

MAID

She's not in the dance.

FATHER

(Energetically) There are so many people. Go look!

MAID

I've already looked!

FATHER

(Tragically) Well, where is she?

BRIDEGROOM

(Entering) Nothing. She's not anywhere.

MOTHER

(To FATHER) What is this? Where is your daughter?

(LEONARDO's WIFE enters)

WIFE

They ran away! They ran away! She and Leonardo! On the horse!
They rode off in each other's arms, like a bolt of lightning!

FATHER

It's not true! My daughter? No!

MOTHER

Your daughter, yes! Born of an evil mother, and him—him,
too! But now she is my son's wife!

BRIDEGROOM

(Entering) Let's go after them! Who has a horse?

MOTHER

Who has a horse? Right now—who has a horse? I'll give you everything I have: my eyes and even my tongue!

VOICE

There's one here!

MOTHER

(To BRIDEGROOM*)* Go! After them!

(He leaves with two YOUNG MEN*)*

No! Don't go! Those people kill quickly and well! But—yes: run! And I'll follow.

FATHER

It can't be her! Maybe she threw herself into the cistern!

MOTHER

Honorable women throw themselves into the water, the decent ones. Not that one! But now she's my son's wife!

(Everyone enters)

Two sides! There are two sides here! My family and yours! Everyone, leave here! Clean the dust from your shoes! We are going to help my son!

(The CROWD *separates into two groups)*

Because he has his people—his cousins from the sea! And all those who came from the interior! Out of here! Along every road! It has come once again—the hour of blood! Two sides! You with yours and me with mine! After them! After them!

CURTAIN

ACT III

SCENE I

(A forest. Night. Great moist tree trunks. A murky atmosphere. Two violins are playing. Three WOODCUTTERS *enter)*

FIRST WOODCUTTER

And have they found them?

SECOND WOODCUTTER

No. But they're searching everywhere.

THIRD WOODCUTTER

They will find them soon.

SECOND WOODCUTTER

Ssshhh!

THIRD WOODCUTTER

What?

SECOND WOODCUTTER

They seem to be closing in on every road at once.

FIRST WOODCUTTER

When the moon comes out, they will see them.

SECOND WOODCUTTER

They should leave them alone.

FIRST WOODCUTTER

The world is wide—everyone can live in it.

THIRD WOODCUTTER

But they will kill them.

SECOND WOODCUTTER

You must follow your heart. They did well to run away.

FIRST WOODCUTTER

They had been lying to each other. But in the end, blood was stronger!

THIRD WOODCUTTER

Blood!

FIRST WOODCUTTER

You must follow the course of your blood.

SECOND WOODCUTTER

But blood that is spilled is soaked up by the earth.

FIRST WOODCUTTER

What of it? Better to be dead with no blood than alive with it festering.

THIRD WOODCUTTER

Be quiet!

FIRST WOODCUTTER

What? Do you hear something?

THIRD WOODCUTTER

I hear the crickets, the frogs, the ambush of the night.

FIRST WOODCUTTER

But you don't hear the horse.

THIRD WOODCUTTER

No.

FIRST WOODCUTTER

Now he must be making love to her.

SECOND WOODCUTTER

Her body was meant for him; his body was meant for her.

THIRD WOODCUTTER

They will track them down and kill them.

FIRST WOODCUTTER

But their blood will have mingled by then! They will be like two empty water jars, like two dry rivers.

SECOND WOODCUTTER

There are many clouds, and it will be easy for the moon not to come out.

THIRD WOODCUTTER

The bridegroom will find them—with the moon or without the moon! I saw him start off—like a raging star! His face, the color of ashes, revealed the fate of his whole family.

FIRST WOODCUTTER

His family of corpses in the middle of the road!

SECOND WOODCUTTER

That's right.

THIRD WOODCUTTER

Do you think they will manage to break through the circle?

SECOND WOODCUTTER

It would be difficult. There are knives and guns for ten leagues around.

THIRD WOODCUTTER

He's riding a good horse . . .

SECOND WOODCUTTER

But he is carrying a woman!

FIRST WOODCUTTER

We are close now.

SECOND WOODCUTTER

A tree with forty branches. We'll soon cut it down.

THIRD WOODCUTTER

Now the moon is coming out. Let's hurry!

(The lights grow brighter at stage left)

FIRST WOODCUTTER

O rising Moon!
Moon of the giant leaves.

SECOND WOODCUTTER

Fill the blood with jasmine!

FIRST WOODCUTTER

O lonely Moon!
Moon of the tender leaves.

SECOND WOODCUTTER

Silver on the face of the bride!

THIRD WOODCUTTER

O evil Moon!
Leave the dark bough for their love!

FIRST WOODCUTTER

O somber Moon!
Leave the dark bough for their love!

(They exit. The MOON *appears through the light at stage left. The* MOON *is a young woodcutter in whiteface. The stage takes on a vivid blue brilliance)*

MOON

I'm a round swan on the river.
I'm the cathedrals' eye.
I'm the false dawn in the treetops.
They will not get away!
Who's hiding there? Who sobs
Beneath the thorns and brambles?
The moon drops down a dagger,
Abandoned in the air—
Ambush of lead that aims to be
The agony of blood.
Let me in! I come, frozen,
Through the walls and windows;
Open your roofs, your breast
Where I can warm myself!
I am cold! My ashes
Of heavy, sleeping metals
Seek the crest of fire
Through the streets and mountains.
But the snow will bear me
Upon its jasper shoulder;
I'll sink beneath the water
Of the frozen ponds.
And so tonight my cheeks
Will fill with crimson blood
And the reeds that huddle
At the wide feet of the wind.
Allow no shade, no shadow—
They will not get away!
I want to enter a breast,
So I can warm myself!
A heart! A heart for me—
Feverish, let it flow
Over the hills of my breast.
Let me in! Oh, let me!
            (To the boughs)
I want no shade. My rays
Must enter everywhere:

Among the darkened trees,
A murmuring of light.
So that tonight I'll have
Sweet blood upon my cheeks
And the reeds that huddle
At the wide feet of the wind.
Who is hiding? Come out, I say!
No! They cannot escape!
I'll make the horse shine bright,
A feverish diamond light!

(The MOON *disappears between the tree trunks, and the stage lights dim again. A very old woman enters, completely covered in flimsy, dark green garments. She is barefoot. Her face can barely be seen under the folds of cloth. This character does not appear on the cast list)*

BEGGAR WOMAN

That moon is gone, and they draw near.
They'll go no farther. The river's whisper
And the whispering trunks of trees will drown
Their screams, their lacerated screams.
Here it will be, and soon. I am so tired!
The coffers open, and clean white sheets
Are waiting upon the bedroom floor
For bodies of men whose throats have been torn.
Let no bird wake. And let the breeze
Gather their moans in the folds of her skirt
And fly with them over the black treetops,
Or bury them deep in the softness of mud.
                    (Impatiently)
That moon, that moon!

(The MOON *appears. The intense blue light returns)*

MOON

                              Now they are near!
Some through the ravine, the other along the river.
I'll shine on the rocks. What do you need?

BEGGAR WOMAN

Nothing.

MOON

The wind blows hard, with a double edge.

BEGGAR WOMAN

Shine on his vest, open the buttons—
Then the daggers will know their way.

MOON

Let them be a long time dying.
Let blood hiss softly through my fingers.
See my ashen valleys waken,
Anxious for this trembling fountain!

BEGGAR WOMAN

We won't let them cross the river. Silence!

MOON

There they come!

(The MOON *exits. The stage lights dim)*

BEGGAR WOMAN

Hurry! Lots of light!
Did you hear me? They cannot escape!

(The BRIDEGROOM *and the* FIRST YOUNG MAN *enter. The* BEGGAR WOMAN *sits down and conceals herself in her shawl)*

BRIDEGROOM

(Entering) This way.

FIRST YOUNG MAN

You won't find them.

BRIDEGROOM

(Forcefully) Yes, I will find them!

FIRST YOUNG MAN

I think they've taken another path.

BRIDEGROOM

No. A moment ago, I heard galloping.

FIRST YOUNG MAN

It must have been another horse.

BRIDEGROOM

(Dramatically) Listen! There is only one horse in the world—and it's this one! Do you understand! If you follow me, follow me without talking!

FIRST YOUNG MAN

I just wish—

BRIDEGROOM

Be quiet! I am sure I'll find them here! See this arm? Well, it is not my arm—it is the arm of my brother and of my father and of everyone in my family who is dead! And it has so much power that it can pull this tree up by the roots if it wants! And let's hurry, because I feel the teeth of my whole family digging into me—here! In a way that makes it impossible for me to breathe easily.

BEGGAR WOMAN

(Whining) Ay!

FIRST YOUNG MAN

Did you hear that?

BRIDEGROOM

Go that way, and circle back.

This is a hunt.

BRIDEGROOM

The greatest there can be!

(The YOUNG MAN *exits. The* BRIDEGROOM *goes rapidly toward the left and stumbles upon the* BEGGAR WOMAN: *Death)*

BEGGAR WOMAN

Ay!

BRIDEGROOM

What do you want?

BEGGAR WOMAN

I am cold!

BRIDEGROOM

Which way are you going?

BEGGAR WOMAN

(Still whining, like a beggar) That way—far away.

BRIDEGROOM

Where are you coming from?

BEGGAR WOMAN

From there. From very far.

BRIDEGROOM

Did you see a man and a woman race by on horseback?

BEGGAR WOMAN

(Uncovering herself) Wait! *(Looks at him)* Beautiful young man! *(She gets up)* But much more beautiful if you were asleep!

BRIDEGROOM

Tell me! Answer! Did you see them?

BEGGAR WOMAN

Wait! What broad shoulders! Why don't you want to be laid out on them, instead of walking around on the soles of such small feet?

BRIDEGROOM

(Shaking her) I asked you if you saw them! Have they passed through here?

BEGGAR WOMAN

(Forcefully) They have not passed! But they are coming down the hill. Don't you hear?

BRIDEGROOM

No.

BEGGAR WOMAN

You don't know the road?

BRIDEGROOM

I will go, whatever it takes!

BEGGAR WOMAN

I will go with you. I know this land.

BRIDEGROOM

(Impatiently) Then let's go! Which way?

BEGGAR WOMAN

(Dramatically) Through there!

(They exit rapidly. Two violins are heard in the distance. They evoke the forest. The WOODCUTTERS return, their axes on their shoulders. They walk slowly between the trunks of the trees)

FIRST WOODCUTTER

Death! Death is coming,
Beneath the giant leaves!

SECOND WOODCUTTER

Don't start the flow of blood!

FIRST WOODCUTTER

Death, lonely death,
Beneath the withered leaves.

THIRD WOODCUTTER

Don't cover the wedding with flowers!

SECOND WOODCUTTER

Death, mournful death,
Leave a green branch for love!

THIRD WOODCUTTER

Death, vicious death,
Leave a green branch for love.

(They each leave as they speak. LEONARDO *and the* BRIDE *enter)*

LEONARDO

Quiet!

BRIDE

From here, I'll go alone!
Leave! I want you to go back!

LEONARDO

Quiet, I said!

BRIDE

With your teeth,
With your hands—however you can—
Take this metal chain from my neck.

Leave me, let me live forsaken,
There in my house made of earth.
And if you do not want to kill me,
As you would kill the smallest snake,
Then put the barrel of your gun
Into my hands, the hands of a bride!
A song of sorrow—burning! burning!
Rises up inside my head!
My tongue is pierced with glass.

LEONARDO

We've taken the step now. Quiet!
Because they follow us closely,
And I must take you with me.

BRIDE

Then it must be by force!

LEONARDO

By force? But which of us went first
Back there? Who led me down the stairs?

BRIDE

I led the way.

LEONARDO

Who untied the horse?

BRIDE

I did. I did. It's true!

LEONARDO

Whose hands
Put spurs upon my boots?

BRIDE

These hands that are yours. They ache
To dig into your flesh

And open each blue vein
To hear your murmuring blood.
I love you! I love you! But leave me!
If I were able to kill you,
I'd wrap you in a shroud
Bordered with violets!
A song of sorrow—burning!
Rises in my head!

LEONARDO

My tongue is pierced with glass!
In order to forget,
I put a wall of stone
Between your house and mine.
It's true! Don't you remember?
Seeing you in the distance,
I'd fill my eyes with sand!
But I would take my horse,
And the horse would go to your door.
The silver pins of your wedding
Were making my blood turn black.
The dream was filling my flesh
With bitter, choking weeds!
Because the blame's not mine!
The blame belongs to the earth
And to the smell that comes
From your breasts and from your braids.

BRIDE

I must be mad! I do not want
To share your bed or food,
But every minute of the day
I long to be with you.
You pull me, and I go along,
And then you push me back.
And helplessly I follow you
Like straw blown on the wind.
I've left a good and honest man,

His family, his house,
In the middle of the wedding,
Still wearing my bridal crown!
But you are the one they will punish,
And I don't want that to be.
Leave me alone! Escape!
No one can help you now.

LEONARDO

The first wild birds of the morning
Are breaking out of the trees.
And now the night is dying
On the sharp edge of the stone.
Let's find a corner of darkness
Where I will love you always,
And I won't care about people
Or the poison that they spread.

(He embraces her tightly)

BRIDE

And I will lie at your feet—
Guarding what you dream—
Naked, watching the fields
   (Dramatically)
As if I were your dog.
Because I am! I look at you:
Your beauty makes me burn!

LEONARDO

Fire is fed by fire.
The same small flame destroys
Two stalks of wheat at once.
Let's go! *(He pulls her)*

BRIDE
  Where are you taking me?

LEONARDO

Somewhere they cannot go,
These men who now surround us—
Where I can look at you!

BRIDE

(Sarcastically)
And show me at the country fairs,
"An Insult to Decent Women"?
So everyone can stare at me,
My wedding sheets unfurled
As if they were my banners?

LEONARDO

I would want to leave you, too,
If I thought like others think!
But wherever you go, I am going.
And you, too. Take one step. Only try!
The moon nails us together.
My loins are fused to your thighs.

(This entire scene is violent, filled with great sensuality)

BRIDE

Listen!

LEONARDO

They're coming!

BRIDE

Run!
It's right for me to die
Here, with my feet in the water
And thorns around my head.
And for the leaves to mourn me:
A lost and fallen maiden!

LEONARDO
Quiet! They're here now!

BRIDE
Go!

LEONARDO
Be still! Don't let them hear us!
You first. Let's go, I say!

(The BRIDE *hesitates)*

BRIDE
Together!

LEONARDO
(Embracing her)
As you wish!
If they tear us apart, it will be
Because I am dead.

BRIDE
And I am dead!

(They exit, their arms around each other)

(The MOON *emerges, very slowly. The stage takes on an intense blue light. The two violins play. Suddenly, their music is cut short by two long, piercing screams. On the second scream, the* BEGGAR WOMAN *appears and stands with her back to the audience. She opens her cloak and remains at center stage, like a great bird with immense wings. The* MOON *stops moving. The curtain descends on complete silence)*

CURTAIN

SCENE 2

(A room with arches and thick walls. At left and right, white stairways. Upstage, a very large arch, and a wall the same color. Even the floor is shining white. This unadorned room has the monumental feeling of a church. There must not be a single gray, a single shadow—not even if required for perspective. TWO GIRLS *dressed in dark blue are unwinding a red* madeja, *a skein of wool.* A LITTLE GIRL *watches)*

FIRST GIRL

Madeja, madeja,
What will you make?

SECOND GIRL

Jasmine clothing,
Crystal paper.
Born at four,
Dead at ten.
The woolen thread
A chain at your feet
A knot that binds
Bitter laurel.

LITTLE GIRL
(Singing)
Did you go to the wedding?

FIRST GIRL

No.

LITTLE GIRL

Neither did I!
What could have happened
In the budding vineyard?
What could have happened
In the olive grove?

How could it happen
That no one returned?
Did you go to the wedding?

SECOND GIRL

We told you: no.

LITTLE GIRL
(Leaving)

Neither did I!

SECOND GIRL

Madeja, madeja,
What will you sing?

FIRST GIRL

Wounds of wax,
The pain of myrtle.
Sleeping by morning,
Watching by night.

LITTLE GIRL
(At the door)

The thread is caught
Upon the flint.
The azure mountains
Let it pass.
It runs and runs,
And then arrives
At the stab of the knife,
The last of the bread.

(She exits)

SECOND GIRL

Madeja, madeja,
What will you say?

The Lover is silent.
Crimson, the Groom.
On the mute riverbank,
I saw them laid out.

(She pauses, staring at the madeja*)*

LITTLE GIRL
(Coming to the door)
The thread runs and runs
It runs to here.
Covered with mud.
I hear them come.
Lifeless bodies,
Ivory sheets.

*(*LEONARDO's WIFE *and* MOTHER-IN-LAW *enter, anguished. The* LITTLE GIRL *exits)*

FIRST GIRL
Are they coming now?

MOTHER-IN-LAW
(Sourly) We don't know.

SECOND GIRL
What can you tell us about the wedding?

FIRST GIRL
Tell me!

MOTHER-IN-LAW
(Dryly) Nothing.

WIFE
I want to return, to know everything.

MOTHER-IN-LAW

(Forcefully)

You: go to your house!
Brave and alone in your house.
You will grow old and you'll weep.
Always, the door will be closed.
Never. Living or dead.
We'll nail down the windows forever.
Let the rains come, and night
Blanket the bitter weeds!

WIFE

What could have happened!

MOTHER-IN-LAW

No matter.

Cover your face with a veil.
Your children are children of yours,
Nothing else matters to you.
You must place a cross made of ashes
On the bed where his pillow has been.

(They exit)

BEGGAR WOMAN

(At the door) A piece of bread, girls!

LITTLE GIRL

Go away!

(The GIRLS *draw together)*

BEGGAR WOMAN

Why?

LITTLE GIRL

Because

You whine. Go away!

FIRST GIRL
Child!

BEGGAR WOMAN
I could have asked you for your eyes!
A cloud of birds follows me. Want one?

LITTLE GIRL
I want to leave!

SECOND GIRL
(To the BEGGAR WOMAN*)* Don't pay attention!

FIRST GIRL
You came along the road by the stream?

BEGGAR WOMAN
I came that way.

FIRST GIRL
(Timidly) Can I ask you—?

BEGGAR WOMAN
I saw them. They'll soon be here. Two torrents,
Still at last among the boulders.
Two men at the feet of the horse.
Dead in the splendor of the night.
(Savoring it)
Dead! Yes, dead!

FIRST GIRL
Quiet, old woman!

BEGGAR WOMAN
Their eyes are broken flowers. Their teeth
Are just two handfuls of frozen snow.
They both fell dead. The bride returns
With bloodstains on her skirt and hair.

Covered with blankets, the bodies come,
Come on the shoulders of tall young men.
That's how it was. Nothing more. It was just.
Over the golden flower—filthy sand.

(She leaves. The GIRLS *bow their heads and start to exit, rhythmically)*

FIRST GIRL

Filthy sand.

SECOND GIRL

Over the golden flower.

LITTLE GIRL

Over the golden flower.
They bring the dead from the stream.
Young and dark, the one.
Young and dark, the other.
The nightingale of shadow
Soars and grieves
Over the golden flower!

(She leaves. The stage is empty. The MOTHER *enters with the* NEIGHBOR, *who is weeping)*

MOTHER

Quiet!

NEIGHBOR

I can't.

MOTHER

Quiet, I said! *(At the doorway)* Is there no one here? *(She puts her hands to her forehead)* My son should be answering me! But my son is now an armful of withered flowers. My son is now a dim voice behind the mountains. *(Angrily, to the* NEIGHBOR*)* Will you be quiet? I want no weeping in this house. Your tears are tears that come only from your eyes, and mine will come when

I am alone—from the soles of my feet, from my roots—and they will burn hotter than blood!

NEIGHBOR

Come to my house—don't stay here.

MOTHER

Here. Here is where I want to be. And at peace. Now everyone is dead. At midnight, I will sleep. I will sleep at last, no longer terrified of guns or knives. Other mothers will be looking out of windows lashed by the rain, to see the faces of their sons. Not me. I will make from my dream a cold ivory dove that will carry camellias of frost over the cemetery. But no! —Not the cemetery, not the cemetery! —A bed of earth, a bed that shelters them and rocks them in the sky.

(A WOMAN *dressed in black enters, goes to the right, and kneels there)*

(To the NEIGHBOR*)* Take your hands from your face. There are terrible days ahead of us. I don't want to see anyone. The earth and me! My tears and me! And these four walls! Oh! Oh! *(She sits down, overcome)*

NEIGHBOR

Have pity on yourself.

MOTHER

(Pushing her hair back) I must be calm. Because the neighbors will be coming, and I don't want them to see how poor I am. How poor! A woman without even one son to touch to her lips!

(The BRIDE *enters, without her orange blossom, wearing a black cape)*

NEIGHBOR

(Looking at the BRIDE *angrily)* Where are you going?

BRIDE

I'm coming here.

MOTHER

(To the NEIGHBOR*)* Who is it?

NEIGHBOR

Don't you recognize her?

MOTHER

That's why I ask who it is. Because I must not recognize her, so I won't dig my teeth into her neck! You vile serpent! *(She moves threateningly toward the* BRIDE, *then stops. To the* NEIGHBOR*)* You see her? She's there, and she's crying, and I—calm —without tearing her eyes out. I don't understand myself. Could it be that I didn't love my son? But what about her honor? Where is her honor? *(She strikes the* BRIDE, *who falls to the floor)*

NEIGHBOR

My God! *(She tries to separate them)*

BRIDE

(To NEIGHBOR*)* Let her! I have come so she can kill me and I can be buried with them. *(To the* MOTHER*)* But not with your hands—with grappling hooks, with a sickle, and with all your might, until it breaks on my bones. Go ahead! But I want you to know I am unstained. I may be mad, but they can bury me without any man ever having seen himself in the whiteness of my breasts!

MOTHER

Be quiet! Be quiet! What do I care about that?

BRIDE

Because I ran away with another man, I ran away! *(Anguished)* You would have gone, too! I was a woman consumed by fire, covered with open sores inside and out, and your son was a little bit of water from whom I hoped for children, land, health! But the other was a dark river filled with branches that brought close to me the whisper of its rushes and its murmuring song. And I would go with your son, who was like a little boy made of cold water, and the other would send hundreds of birds that blocked my way and left frost on the wounds of this poor, wasted woman, a girl caressed by fire! I didn't want to! Listen to me! I didn't want to! Your son was what I wanted, and I have not deceived him. But the arm of the other dragged me—like the surge of the sea, like a mule butting me with his head—and would have dragged me always, always, always! Even if I were old and all the sons of your son held me by the hair!

(A NEIGHBOR *enters)*

MOTHER

It's not her fault. Nor mine! *(Sarcastically)* Whose is it, then? Loose, weak, indecent woman—who throws off her bridal crown to go looking for a piece of a bed warmed by another woman!

BRIDE

Stop it! Stop it! Take your revenge on me! Here I am! See how soft my neck is? It will be easier than cutting a dahlia from your garden. But that, no! Honorable, as honorable as a newborn child! And strong enough to prove it to you! Light the fire! We'll put our hands in it—you, for your son; me, for my body! You'll take yours out first!

(Another NEIGHBOR *comes in)*

MOTHER

What do I care about your honor? What do I care about your death? What do I care about anything at all? Blessed be the fields of wheat, because my sons lie under them. Blessed be the rain, because it wets the faces of the dead. Blessed be God who lays us down together to rest.

(Another NEIGHBOR *enters)*

BRIDE

Let me weep with you.

MOTHER

Weep. But at the door.

(LITTLE GIRL *enters; the* BRIDE *remains at the door, the* MOTHER
at the center of the stage)

WIFE
(Enters, goes to the left)
He was a handsome horseman
And now he's a bank of snow.
He rode through the fairs and mountains
And into the arms of love.
And now the moss of night
Is a crown around his forehead.

MOTHER

My child, my son, my sunflower,
Mirror of the earth.
Upon your chest a cross
Of bitter oleander—
A sheet to cover you
With shining, silken strands.
And water forms a sob
Between your quiet hands.

WIFE

Oh, the four young men
Who come with weary shoulders!

BRIDE

Oh, the fair young men
Who carry death through the air!

MOTHER

Neighbors!

LITTLE GIRL
(At the doorway)
They're bringing them now.

MOTHER

It's the same—
The Cross! The Cross!

WOMEN

Sweet nails,
Sweet Cross,
Sweet Name—
Jesus.

MOTHER

May the Cross protect the dead and the living!

Neighbors, with a knife,
With a little knife,
On a fated day, between two and three o'clock,
Two men killed each other over love.
With a knife, with a little knife
That scarcely fits the hand,
But penetrates precisely
Through the astonished flesh
To stop exactly at the place
Where, trembling and entangled,
Lies the dark root of the scream.

BRIDE

And this is a knife,
A little knife
That scarcely fits the hand,
Fish without scales or river.
So on a fated day, between two and three o'clock,
With this knife
Two men are left dead,
With their lips turning yellow.

MOTHER

And it scarcely fits the hand,
But penetrates so coldly
Through the astonished flesh,
And stops there—at the place
Where, trembling and entangled,
Lies the dark root of the scream.

(The NEIGHBORS, *kneeling on the ground, weep)*

CURTAIN

YERMA

A TRAGIC POEM

IN THREE ACTS

AND SIX SCENES

Cast of Characters

YERMA

JUAN

VICTOR

MARIA

DOLORES

TWO SISTERS-IN-LAW

PAGAN OLD WOMAN

MALE

FEMALE

BOY

SHEPHERD

CHILD

SIX WASHERWOMEN

TWO GIRLS

TWO WOMEN

TWO OLD WOMEN

THREE MEN

SEVEN YOUNG GIRLS

CHILDREN

ACT I

SCENE I

(When the curtain rises, YERMA *is asleep with a sewing basket at her feet. There is a strange, dreamlike light. A* SHEPHERD *tiptoes in, staring at* YERMA. *He leads a* CHILD *dressed in white by the hand. The clock strikes. When the* SHEPHERD *exits, the light changes to the cheerfulness of a spring morning.* YERMA *wakes up)*

VOICE SINGING
(Offstage)
Nana, Nana, Nana,
Nana, you will see—
We will build a little nest,
And that's where we will be.

YERMA

Juan, do you hear me? Juan!

JUAN

(Offstage) Coming.

YERMA

It's time.

JUAN

(Entering) Have the oxen gone by?

YERMA

Yes, they have.

JUAN

See you later. *(He starts to leave)*

YERMA

Don't you want a glass of milk?

JUAN

What for?

YERMA

You work hard, and you aren't strong enough for so much work.

JUAN

When men stay thin, they get as strong as steel.

YERMA

But not you. When we got married, you were different. Now your face is pale—as if the sun never touched it. I wish you'd go down to the river and swim, and go up on the roof when the rain is pouring down on our house. Twenty-four months we've been married, and you keep growing sadder, thinner— as if you were growing backwards.

JUAN

Have you finished?

YERMA

(Standing up) Don't take it wrong. If I were sick, I'd want you to take care of me. "My wife is sick. I'm going to kill this lamb to make a good meat stew." "My wife is sick. I'm going to save this chicken fat to rub on her chest." "I'm going to take her this sheepskin to wrap around her feet when it snows." That's the way I am. That's why I take care of you.

JUAN

And I'm grateful.

YERMA

But you won't let yourself be taken care of.

JUAN

Because there's nothing wrong with me. You're just imagining all these things. I work hard. Every year I will get older.

YERMA

Every year . . . You and I will go on living here every
year . . .

JUAN

(Smiling) Of course. And very peacefully. The work is going
well, and we have no children to waste money on.

YERMA

We have no children . . . Juan!

JUAN

Yes.

YERMA

Do you think I don't love you?

JUAN

You love me.

YERMA

I know girls who trembled and cried before they got into bed
with their husbands. Did I cry the first time I went to bed with
you? Wasn't I singing as I lifted the linen sheets? Didn't I say to
you, "These sheets smell just like apples!"

JUAN

That's what you said.

YERMA

My mother cried because I didn't mind leaving her. And it was
true. No one was ever happier to get married. And yet . . .

JUAN

Quiet!

YERMA

And yet . . .

Stop it! It's hard enough for me to be hearing all the time—

Don't! Don't keep telling me what people are saying! I can see with my own eyes that's it's not true—that when the rain falls on the rocks, they soften and make the wild mustard grow, and people say it's useless. "That plant is useless." But I can clearly see its yellow blossoms moving in the breeze.

You have to wait!

Yes! Wanting! (*Taking the initiative,* YERMA *embraces her husband and kisses him*)

If you need anything, let me know, and I'll bring it. You know I don't like you going out.

I never go out.

You're better off here.

Yes.

The streets are for people with nothing to do.

(*Somberly*) Of course.

(Her husband exits and YERMA *starts toward her sewing, stroking her stomach with her hand. Stretching her arms, she yawns gracefully and sits down to sew)*

(Singing)
Where are you coming from, love, my child?
"From the ice at the mountain's crest."
What do you need, my love, my child?
"To be warmed by the cloth of your dress."
(She threads her needle)
Let the trees lift their branches up to the sun!
Let the fountains leap, and the river run!
(Then, as if speaking to a child)
The dog is barking, out in the patio.
The wind in the trees is singing there.
The oxen follow the herder lowing,
And the moon is weaving braids in my hair.
What do you ask for, child, from so far?
(She pauses)
"For the mountains of your white breast."
Let the trees lift their branches up to the sun!
Let the fountains leap, and the river run!
(She sews)
I tell you, my child—it's true, it's true:
I am broken and torn for you.
My womb aches for you—
An empty cradle, craving you.
When, my child, are you going to come?
(She pauses)
"When your flesh smells like jasmine."
Let the trees lift their branches up to the sun!
Let the fountains leap, and the river run!

*(*YERMA *goes on singing.* MARIA *enters through the door with a bundle of clothes)*

Where are you coming from?

MARIA

From the store.

YERMA

From the store, so early?

MARIA

If I had my way, I'd have been waiting at the door when they opened. You'll never guess what I bought!

YERMA

You probably bought coffee for breakfast, sugar, some bread.

MARIA

No! I bought lace, three spools of thread, ribbon, and colored yarn to make tassels. My husband had some money put aside and he himself gave it to me.

YERMA

Are you going to make a blouse?

MARIA

No, it's because—you know?

YERMA

What?

MARIA

Because it's finally happened. *(She lowers her head.)*

(YERMA rises and gazes at her in admiration)

YERMA

In five months!

MARIA

Yes.

YERMA

Can you tell it's there?

MARIA

Of course.

YERMA

(With curiosity) And what are you feeling?

MARIA

I don't know. Queasy.

YERMA

Queasy? *(Holding on to her)* But—when it happened . . . ? Tell me! You got carried away.

MARIA

Yes, carried away . . .

YERMA

You must have been singing, yes? I sing. You—tell me—

MARIA

Don't ask me. Have you ever held a live bird tight in your hand?

YERMA

Yes.

MARIA

Well, it's the same—but in your blood.

YERMA

How beautiful. *(She stares at her in wonder)*

MARIA

I'm in a daze. I don't know anything.

YERMA

About what?

MARIA

About what I should do! I'll ask my mother.

YERMA

What for? She's old now and she must have forgotten all that. Don't move around too much, and when you breathe, breathe as softly as if you had a rose between your teeth.

MARIA

Listen, they say that later on he pushes you gently with his little legs.

YERMA

And that's when you love him the most—when at last you say, "My son!"

MARIA

In the middle of all this, I feel embarrassed.

YERMA

What did your husband say?

MARIA

Nothing.

YERMA

Does he love you very much?

MARIA

He doesn't tell me so, but he comes close to me and his eyes quiver like two green leaves.

YERMA

Did he know when you . . .

Yes.

YERMA

How could he tell?

MARIA

I don't know. But on our wedding night he kept saying it, over and over, with his mouth pressed to my cheek—so many times that I feel as if my baby is a fiery dove that he slipped into my ear.

YERMA

You are lucky!

MARIA

But you know more about this than I do.

YERMA

What good does it do me?

MARIA

That's true! Why is that? Of all the girls that got married when you did, you're the only one who . . .

YERMA

That's how it is. Of course, there's still time. It took Elena three years, and in my mother's day it used to take some women much longer. But two years and twenty days, like me, is too long to wait! I don't think it's fair for me to waste away here. Many nights I go out on the patio barefoot, to feel the earth under my feet, and I don't know why. If I go on like this, I'll come to a bad end.

MARIA

Now, look here, child! You are talking like an old woman. Listen to me. You can't complain about these things. My mother's sister had one after fourteen years—and if you could have seen the beauty of that child!

YERMA

(*Eagerly*) What did he do?

MARIA

He howled like a young bull, as loud as a thousand cicadas singing at once! And he wet all over us, and pulled on our braids! And when he was four months old, he covered our faces with scratches!

YERMA

(*Laughing*) But those things don't hurt!

MARIA

I'll let you know—

YERMA

Bah! I've seen my sister nursing her baby with her breast covered with scratches and it was very painful. But it was good pain—fresh, new, necessary for health.

MARIA

They say children cause a lot of suffering.

YERMA

That's a lie! Mothers who say that are weaklings, complainers! Why do they have them? Having a child is no bed of roses! We have to suffer for them to grow up. It must drain half our blood. But that's good, healthy, beautiful! Every woman has enough blood for four or five children, and if she doesn't have them, it turns to poison, as it will with me.

MARIA

I don't know what's wrong with me.

YERMA

I always heard that the first time is frightening.

MARIA

(Timidly) We'll see . . . Since you sew so well . . .

YERMA

(Taking the bundle) Give it to me. I'll cut two little suits for you.
What is this?

MARIA

Those are the diapers.

YERMA

Good. (She sits down)

MARIA

Then . . . I'll see you later. (She approaches YERMA, who places
both hands lovingly on her belly)

YERMA

Don't go running on the cobblestones.

MARIA

Goodbye! (She kisses her and goes out)

YERMA

Come back soon.

(YERMA is left as we found her at the beginning. She takes the scissors
and starts to cut. VICTOR enters)

Hello, Victor!

VICTOR

(He is intense and grave) Where is Juan?

YERMA

In the fields . . .

VICTOR

What are you making?

YERMA

I'm cutting some diapers.

VICTOR

(Smiling) Good for you!

YERMA

(Laughing) I'm going to edge them with lace.

VICTOR

If it's a girl, she'll have your name.

YERMA

(Trembling) What?

VICTOR

I'm happy for you.

YERMA

(Almost choking) No—they're not for me! They're for Maria's baby.

VICTOR

Well then, let's see you follow her example. This house needs a child.

YERMA

(In anguish) It does!

VICTOR

Then go ahead! Tell your husband to think less about his work. He wants to save money and he will, but who will he leave it to when he dies? I'm going out to the sheep. Tell Juan to pick up the two he bought from me. And as for the other—tell him to dig deeper! *(He exits, smiling)*

YERMA

(Passionately) That's it! Much deeper!

I tell you, my child, it's true, it's true!
I am broken and torn for you!
My womb aches for you,
An empty cradle, craving you.
When, my child, are you going to come?
"When your flesh smells like jasmine."

(YERMA rises pensively and goes to the spot where VICTOR stood. She takes a deep breath as if inhaling mountain air, then goes to the other side of the room as if seeking something, and from there returns to sit down and pick up her sewing again. She begins to sew, but stops and stares at one spot)

CURTAIN

SCENE 2

(In the fields. YERMA enters. She is carrying a basket. The FIRST OLD WOMAN enters)

YERMA

Good morning!

PAGAN OLD WOMAN

And a good one to you, pretty miss! Where are you going?

YERMA

I've just taken my husband his lunch. He's working in the olive groves.

PAGAN OLD WOMAN

Have you been married long?

YERMA

Three years.

PAGAN OLD WOMAN

Do you have children?

YERMA

No.

PAGAN OLD WOMAN

Bah! You will have.

YERMA

(Eagerly) Do you think so?

PAGAN OLD WOMAN

Why not? *(She sits down)* I just took my husband his lunch, too.
He's an old man. He still works. I have nine children, like nine
shining suns, but since none of them is a girl, here I am, running
from one place to another.

YERMA

You live on the other side of the river.

PAGAN OLD WOMAN

Yes, over by the windmills. Who is your family?

YERMA

I'm the daughter of Enrique the shepherd.

PAGAN OLD WOMAN

Ah! Enrique the shepherd! I knew him! Good people. Get out
of bed, work hard, eat some bread, and die. No games, no
nothing! Rest and repose—that's for other people. Creatures of
silence. I could have married one of your uncles! But no! I have

always been a woman with her skirts in the air! I went straight for the slice of melon, the fiesta, the sugar bun! I've often stuck my head out the door at daybreak, thinking I heard the sound of a guitar coming and going—but it was only the breeze! *(She laughs)* You are going to laugh at me. I've had two husbands and fourteen children. Five died, and in spite of that, I'm not sad and I'd like to live a lot longer! That's what I say! Fig trees—how long they last! Houses—how long they last! And only us, confounded women, we are ground to dust by anything at all!

YERMA

I'd like to ask you a question.

PAGAN OLD WOMAN

You would? *(She looks at her)* I already know what you're going to say. It's not possible to talk about these things. *(She gets up)*

YERMA

(Detaining her) Why not? It's given me confidence to hear you speak. For some time, I've been wanting to have a talk with an older woman. Because I want to know. Yes! You will tell me . . .

PAGAN OLD WOMAN

What?

YERMA

(Lowering her voice) What you know. Why am I dry? Am I going to spend my best years feeding birds and hanging starched curtains in my window? No! You must tell me what I have to do, and I'll do whatever it is, even if I have to stick needles in the most sensitive part of my eyes!

PAGAN OLD WOMAN

Me? I don't know anything! I used to lie on my back and begin to sing. The children came like water. Ah! Could anyone say you don't have a beautiful body? Just step out the door, and down the street a horse will whinny! Oh, leave me alone, child! Don't make me talk. I have a lot of ideas I don't want to talk about.

YERMA

Why not? With my husband, I don't talk about anything else.

PAGAN OLD WOMAN

Tell me—do you like your husband?

YERMA

What?

PAGAN OLD WOMAN

Do you love him? Do you want to be with him?

YERMA

I don't know.

PAGAN OLD WOMAN

Don't you tremble when he comes near you? Don't you feel that you're dreaming when he brings his lips close to yours? Tell me.

YERMA

No. I have never felt like that.

PAGAN OLD WOMAN

Never? Not even when you danced?

YERMA

(Recalling) Perhaps. One time . . . Victor . . .

PAGAN OLD WOMAN

Go on.

YERMA

. . . took me by the waist, and I couldn't say anything to him because I couldn't talk. Another time, this same Victor, fourteen years old—he was a strapping young shepherd—took me in his arms to help me over a ditch and I began to tremble so hard my teeth rattled! But I've always been shy.

PAGAN OLD WOMAN

What about with your husband . . . ?

YERMA

My husband is another matter. My father brought him to me and I accepted him. Happily! That's the simple truth! From the first day we were engaged, I began to think about having children. And I saw myself reflected in his eyes. But very tiny, very manageable—as if I were my own daughter.

PAGAN OLD WOMAN

Just the opposite of me! Perhaps that's why you haven't had a baby yet. Men should be enjoyed, my child! They should undo our braids and give us water to drink from their own mouths. That's what makes the world go round!

YERMA

Yours, but not mine. I have so many dreams, and I'm sure that my son will make those dreams come true. For his sake, I gave myself to my husband, and I keep giving myself to make sure he's on the way—but never for my own pleasure!

PAGAN OLD WOMAN

And the result is, you're empty!

YERMA

No, not empty—I'm filling up with hate! Tell me: is it my fault? Must you look for a man to be a man, nothing more? Then, what are you going to think when he leaves you lying in bed with sad eyes, staring at the ceiling, while he turns over and goes to sleep? Should I lie there thinking about him, or about what can come shining out of my breast? I don't know, but you tell me, I beg you! (*She kneels*)

PAGAN OLD WOMAN

Oh, what a flower in full bloom! What a beautiful creature you are! Leave me alone! Don't make me talk anymore. I don't want to talk to you anymore! It's a question of honor and I don't belittle anyone's honor! You'll find out. Anyway, you shouldn't be so childish!

YERMA

(Sadly) All doors are closed to girls like me, who grow up in the country. Everything is half said, hushed up, because they say we're not supposed to know about such things. And you, too—you, too, keep silent and walk off with the air of a doctor—knowing everything, but denying it to someone who is dying of thirst.

PAGAN OLD WOMAN

I would talk to another woman who was calmer. Not to you! I'm old, and I know what I'm saying.

YERMA

Then God help me!

PAGAN OLD WOMAN

Not God. I never cared for God. When are you going to realize that he doesn't exist? It's men who have to help you!

YERMA

But why are you telling me this, why?

PAGAN OLD WOMAN

(Leaving) Though there should be a God, if only a little one, to throw thunderbolts at men whose rotten seed dams up the joys of the fields!

YERMA

I don't understand what you are trying to tell me.

Well, *I* understand! Don't feel sad. Keep your hopes up. You're
still very young. What do you expect me to do?

(She leaves. TWO YOUNG WOMEN *appear)*

FIRST GIRL

Wherever we go, we keep running into people!

YERMA

The men are all out working in the olive groves, and you have
to take them something to eat. No one stays home except the
old people.

SECOND GIRL

Are you going back to the village?

YERMA

That's where I'm going.

FIRST GIRL

I'm in a big hurry. I left my little boy asleep and there's no one
home.

YERMA

Then get going, woman! Children can't be left alone. Are there
pigs at your house?

FIRST GIRL

No, but you're right. I'll hurry.

YERMA

Go! That's how things can happen! Surely you left him locked
in?

FIRST GIRL

Of course.

YERMA

Yes, but you don't realize what a small child is like. Something that seems so harmless to us could kill him! A tiny needle, a sip of water.

FIRST GIRL

You're right! I'll run. I never really think of such things. *(She exits)*

YERMA

Go!

SECOND GIRL

If you had four or five, you wouldn't talk like that.

YERMA

Why not? Even if I had forty!

SECOND GIRL

Anyway, since you and I don't have any, we live more peacefully.

YERMA

Not me.

SECOND GIRL

I do! What a nuisance! On the other hand, my mother does nothing but give me herbs to make me pregnant, and in October we're going to see the Saint—the one who gives babies to any girl who begs eagerly. My mother will beg. Not me!

YERMA

Why did you get married?

SECOND GIRL

Because they married me off. Everybody gets married! If we go on like this, no one will be left single except the children! Well, anyway—the fact is, a girl gets married long before she goes to the church. But the old women are dead set on all this. I'm nineteen years old and I don't like to cook or clean. Well, now I have to spend the whole day doing things I don't like! And what for? Why is it necessary for my husband to be my husband? We did the same thing when we were engaged that we do now. Old people's foolishness!

YERMA

Hush! Don't say such things!

SECOND GIRL

You'll call me crazy, too! Crazy, crazy! *(She laughs)* I can tell you the one thing I've learned in life: All the people are stuck in their houses doing things they don't like. You're better off out in the middle of the street! Sometimes I go down to the river, sometimes I climb up and ring the church bells, and sometimes I drink a little anisette.

YERMA

You're a child.

SECOND GIRL

Of course, but I'm not crazy! *(She laughs)*

YERMA

Doesn't your mother live up at the top of the village?

SECOND GIRL

Yes.

YERMA

In the last house?

SECOND GIRL

Yes.

YERMA

What's her name?

Dolores. Why do you ask?

No reason.

You must have some reason.

I don't know . . . People say . . .

Whatever . . . Look, I'm going to take my husband his food. *(Laughs)* Isn't that something? It's too bad I can't say "my sweetheart," isn't it? *(Laughs)* Here goes the crazy one! *(She leaves, laughing happily)* Goodbye.

(Singing)
Why are you sleeping alone, shepherd?
Why are you sleeping alone, shepherd?
My blanket is wool.
My blanket is warm.
Why are you sleeping alone, shepherd?

(Listening)
Why are you sleeping alone, shepherd?
My blanket is wool.
My blanket is warm.

Your quilt of dark stone, shepherd.
Your shirt of frost, shepherd.
Gray winter reeds
Your bed at night.
The needles from the oak, shepherd,

Underneath your pillow, shepherd.
And if you hear a woman's voice,
It's the broken voice of water.
Shepherd, shepherd.
What does the mountain want, shepherd?
There are bitter weeds on the hill.
What child is killing you?
There are sharp thorns on the hill.

(YERMA *starts to go, but meets* VICTOR *as he enters*)

VICTOR

(Cheerfully) Where is this beauty going?

YERMA

Was that you singing?

VICTOR

It was.

YERMA

And so well! I never heard you sing before.

VICTOR

No?

YERMA

What a strong voice! Like a gush of water filling your whole mouth.

VICTOR

I'm a happy person.

YERMA

That's true.

VICTOR

As you are sad.

YERMA

I'm not a sad person, but I have enough reason to be.

VICTOR

And your husband is sadder than you are.

YERMA

Yes, he is. That's his nature.

VICTOR

He was always like that.

(He pauses. YERMA sits down)

You came to bring his dinner?

YERMA

Yes. *(She looks at him.)*

(Pause)

What do you have there? *(Pointing to his face)*

VICTOR

Where?

YERMA

(Rising and approaching VICTOR) Here—on your cheek. Like a burn.

VICTOR

It's nothing.

YERMA

To me, it looks like . . . *(Pause)*

VICTOR

It must be the sun.

Perhaps.

(Pause. The silence deepens, and with no outward sign, an intense struggle between the two begins)

(Trembling) Do you hear that?

What?

Don't you hear crying?

(Listening) No.

I thought I heard a child crying.

Yes?

Close by. Crying as if he were drowning!

There are always lots of children around here who come to steal fruit.

No. It was a baby's voice.

(Pause)

I don't hear anything.

YERMA

It must be my imagination. *(She stares at him.* VICTOR *stares back, then slowly turns away as if afraid)*

*(*JUAN *enters)*

JUAN

What are you still doing here?

YERMA

Talking.

VICTOR

Stay well! *(He leaves)*

JUAN

You should be at home.

YERMA

I stopped for a moment.

JUAN

I don't understand what kept you.

YERMA

I heard the birds singing.

JUAN

Oh, fine! That's how you start people talking!

YERMA

(Firmly) Juan, what are you thinking?

JUAN

I'm not talking about you. I'm talking about other people.

YERMA

To hell with other people!

JUAN

Don't swear! It's ugly in a woman.

YERMA

How I wish I *were* a woman!

JUAN

Let's stop this conversation. Go home! *(Pause)*

YERMA

Very well. Should I expect you?

JUAN

No. I'll be watering the crops all night. We've had little rain, and it's my turn until sunrise. And I have to keep people from stealing our water. You go to bed and go to sleep!

YERMA

(Dramatically) I'll go to sleep! *(She leaves)*

CURTAIN

ACT 2

SCENE I

(The women of the town are doing their washing at the falls in the river, sitting on its various levels. They are singing)

ALL

In the icy stream,
I wash your sash.
Warmer than a jasmine
Is your laugh.

FIRST WASHERWOMAN

I don't like to gossip.

THIRD WASHERWOMAN

But we all gossip here.

FOURTH WASHERWOMAN

And there's no harm in it.

FIFTH WASHERWOMAN

A woman who wants a good reputation has to earn it.

FOURTH WASHERWOMAN

I planted some thyme seeds.
See how they grew!
If you want a good name,
Take care what you do!

(They laugh)

FIFTH WASHERWOMAN

That's what they say!

But you never really know.

We do know her husband has brought his two sisters to live with them.

The old maids?

Yes. They used to have the job of keeping an eye on the church. Now they'll be keeping an eye on their sister-in-law! I wouldn't be able to live with them!

Why?

Because they are frightening! Like those enormous leaves that suddenly sprout up out of graves. They're smeared with wax! Plugged up inside! They probably cook their food in kerosene!

Are they already at the house?

Since yesterday. The husband is going out to his fields again.

Can I just know what happened?

She spent the night before last sitting on the doorstep, in spite of the cold!

But why?

FOURTH WASHERWOMAN
It's hard for her to stay in the house!

FIFTH WASHERWOMAN
These barren women are like that. When they could be making lace or apple preserves, they like to go up on the roof or walk barefoot along some river!

FIRST WASHERWOMAN
Who are you to say such things? She has no children, but that's not her fault!

FOURTH WASHERWOMAN
You have children if you *want* to have them! These spoiled, weak, lazy women were never meant to have wrinkles on their bellies!

(They laugh)

THIRD WASHERWOMAN
They put on face powder and rouge, and they wear a sprig of oleander in pursuit of a man who is not their husband!

FIFTH WASHERWOMAN
Nothing could be truer!

FIRST WASHERWOMAN
But have any of you seen her with another man?

FOURTH WASHERWOMAN
We haven't, but other people have!

FIRST WASHERWOMAN
Always other people!

FIFTH WASHERWOMAN
They say it happened on two occasions.

And what were they doing?

Talking.

Talking is not a sin!

There's something in this world called a "look." My mother used to say that. A woman doesn't look at roses the same way she looks at a man's thighs. She "looks" at him!

But at who?

At someone, do you hear? *You* find out. Or do I have to say it louder?

(Laughter)

And when she's not looking at him, because she's alone, because he's not right there in front of her, she has his picture in her mind's eye.

That's a lie!

(There is an uproar)

What about the husband?

The husband acts like he's deaf. He does nothing, like a lizard in the sun.

(They laugh)

FIRST WASHERWOMAN

All this could be straightened out if they had children.

SECOND WASHERWOMAN

All this is what happens to people who don't accept their fate.

FOURTH WASHERWOMAN

Every hour that passes makes that house more like hell! All day long, without ever speaking to each other, she and his sisters whitewash the walls, scour the copper, scrub the windows, polish the floors! And the more that house sparkles, the more like an inferno it becomes!

FIRST WASHERWOMAN

It's his fault, his! If a man can't give his wife children, he'd better keep an eye on her.

FOURTH WASHERWOMAN

It's her fault. She has a tongue that could sharpen knives!

FIRST WASHERWOMAN

What the devil has got into your head to make you talk like that?

FOURTH WASHERWOMAN

Who gave your mouth permission to give me advice?

SECOND WASHERWOMAN

Be quiet!

(Laughter)

FIRST WASHERWOMAN

I'd like to string your muttering tongues on a knitting needle!

SECOND WASHERWOMAN

Shut up!

FOURTH WASHERWOMAN

And me, the tits of hypocrites!

SECOND WASHERWOMAN

Hush! Don't you see his sisters are coming this way?

(They whisper together) YERMA's *two* SISTERS-IN-LAW *enter.*
They're wearing mourning. In the silence, they begin to wash their
clothes. There is the sound of sheep bells)

FIRST WASHERWOMAN

Are the shepherds going now?

THIRD WASHERWOMAN

Yes, now all the flocks will be leaving.

FOURTH WASHERWOMAN

(Inhaling) I love the smell of sheep.

THIRD WASHERWOMAN

You do?

FOURTH WASHERWOMAN

And why not? The smell of what's yours! Just as I like the smell
of the red clay the river brings in the winter.

THIRD WASHERWOMAN

What strange ideas!

FIFTH WASHERWOMAN

(Looking out) The flocks are all leaving together.

FOURTH WASHERWOMAN

It's a flood of wool! Sweeping over everything! If the green wheat
knew what was coming, how it would tremble!

THIRD WASHERWOMAN

Look at them run! Like enemy troops!

Now they're all out. Not one is missing.

Let's see . . . no . . . Yes, yes, one is missing!

FIFTH WASHERWOMAN
Which?

FOURTH WASHERWOMAN
Victor's.

(The two SISTERS-IN-LAW *sit up and look out)*

FOURTH WASHERWOMAN
(Singing)
In the icy stream,
I wash your sash.
Warmer than a jasmine
Is your laugh.
I want to live
In the tiny snowdrift
Of that jasmine.

FIRST WASHERWOMAN
Alas, for the wife who is dry!
Alas, for the wife with breasts of sand!

FIFTH WASHERWOMAN
Tell me if your husband
Still has seed
To send the water singing
Through your shift.

FOURTH WASHERWOMAN
Your shift is a boat
Of silver and wind
On the edge of the stream.

THIRD WASHERWOMAN
I come to the river to wash
The clothes of my son,
To teach the crystal waters
To shine, to run!

SECOND WASHERWOMAN
He's coming from the mountain,
My husband, to eat.
He's bringing me a rosebud,
I will give him three.

FIFTH WASHERWOMAN
He's coming from the lowland,
My husband, to sup.
He's bringing me hot embers,
Which I will cover up.

FOURTH WASHERWOMAN
He's coming on the breezes,
My husband, to bed.
My gillyflowers are crimson.
His gillyflower is red.

THIRD WASHERWOMAN
Join together flower with flower
When summer dries the reaper's blood.

FOURTH WASHERWOMAN
Open your womb to sleepless birds
When winter trembles at the door.

FIRST WASHERWOMAN
We must moan on our bed sheets!

FOURTH WASHERWOMAN
And we must sing!

FIFTH WASHERWOMAN

When a man is bringing
The crown and the bread.

FOURTH WASHERWOMAN

Because our arms will interlace!

FIFTH WASHERWOMAN

Because the light bursts in our throats!

FOURTH WASHERWOMAN

Because the green stalk becomes sweet.

FIFTH WASHERWOMAN

And tents of the wind cover the mountain.

(SIXTH WASHERWOMAN *appears from the top of the falls*)

SIXTH WASHERWOMAN

So that a child can fuse
Crystal shards of dawn.

FOURTH WASHERWOMAN

And our body has
Branches of raging coral.

FIFTH WASHERWOMAN

So that there will be oarsmen
On the waters of the sea.

FIRST WASHERWOMAN

A little child, a child!

SECOND WASHERWOMAN

And doves open their wings and beaks.

THIRD WASHERWOMAN

A child that sobs, a son!

FOURTH WASHERWOMAN
And the men push forward
Like wounded stags.

FIFTH WASHERWOMAN
Joyful, joyful, joyful!
The round womb under the nightgown.

SECOND WASHERWOMAN
Joyful, joyful, joyful!
The navel, tender chalice of wonder.

FIRST WASHERWOMAN
Alas, for the wife who is dry!
Alas, for the wife with breasts of sand!

FOURTH WASHERWOMAN
Let her shine!

FIFTH WASHERWOMAN
Let her run!

FOURTH WASHERWOMAN
Let her shine again!

THIRD WASHERWOMAN
Let her sing!

SECOND WASHERWOMAN
Let her hide!

THIRD WASHERWOMAN
And let her sing again!

SIXTH WASHERWOMAN
The new dawn that my child
Is wearing on his apron.

(In chorus)

In the icy stream
I wash your sash.
Warmer than a jasmine
Is your laugh.
Ha, ha, ha!

(They move the pieces of laundry in rhythm, and beat them)

CURTAIN

SCENE 2

*(YERMA's house. It is growing late. JUAN is seated. The two
SISTERS-IN-LAW are standing)*

JUAN

You say she went out a little while ago?

(The OLDER SISTER-IN-LAW nods her assent)

She must be at the fountain. But you *know* I don't like her to
go out alone.

(Pause)

You can set the table.

(The YOUNGER SISTER-IN-LAW exits)

I really earn the bread I eat! *(To his SISTER)* Yesterday I had a
hard day. I was pruning the apple trees and by the end of the
afternoon I began to think—why am I working so hard if I can't
even put one apple in my mouth? I'm fed up! *(He passes his hand
over his face. Pause)* She hasn't come. One of you should always
go with her! That's why you're here, eating at my table and

drinking my wine! My work is in the fields, but my honor is here. And my honor is yours, as well.

(*The* SISTER-IN-LAW *bows her head*)

Don't take me wrong.

(YERMA *enters carrying two pitchers. She stops in the doorway*)

Have you been to the fountain?

YERMA

Yes, so we could have fresh water with our dinner.

(*The* YOUNGER SISTER-IN-LAW *exits*)

How are things in the fields?

(YERMA *sets down the pitchers. Pause*)

JUAN

I spent yesterday pruning trees.

YERMA

Will you be staying?

JUAN

I have to take care of the flock. You know that's the owner's job.

YERMA

I know it very well. Don't say it again!

JUAN

Every man has his work.

YERMA

And every woman, hers! I'm not asking you to stay. I have

everything I need here. Your sisters watch over me very well. Here I eat fresh bread and cheese and roast lamb, and in the mountains your sheep graze on grass washed with dew. I think you can live in peace.

JUAN

To live in peace, you have to be at peace!

YERMA

And you are not.

JUAN

I am not.

YERMA

Change your way of thinking!

JUAN

Don't you know the way I think? The sheep in the pens, and the women in their houses. You're out too much! Haven't you always heard me say that?

YERMA

You're right! The women in their houses. If the houses are not tombs! If chairs get broken, and linen sheets wear out from being used! But not here! Every night, when I get into bed, the bed seems to be newer, shinier, as if it had just been brought from the city.

JUAN

You yourself admit that I have reason to complain! That I have reason to be on my guard.

YERMA

On your guard against what? I don't do anything to hurt you! I am always submissive to you, and whatever I suffer, I keep to myself. And each day that goes by will be worse. Let's stop talking! I'll carry my cross the best I can, just don't ask me any questions! If I could suddenly become old, with a mouth like a crushed flower, then I could smile at you and share a life with you. Now—now leave me to my agony!

JUAN

You're talking in a way I don't understand. I deprive you of nothing! I send to nearby towns for things you like. I have my faults, but I want to have peace and quiet with you. I want to be able to sleep when I'm away and to know that you're sleeping, too!

YERMA

But I don't sleep, I can't sleep!

JUAN

Is there something you need? Tell me. Answer me!

YERMA

(Meaningfully, staring at her husband) Yes, I need something!

(Pause)

JUAN

Always the same! It's been more than five years now! I've almost forgotten about it.

YERMA

But I'm not you! Men have another life—their flocks, their orchards, their conversations! Women only have their children and caring for their children.

JUAN

Everyone is not the same. Why don't you take in one of your brother's children? I wouldn't be against it.

YERMA

I don't want to take care of other people's children! I think my arms would freeze, just holding them!

JUAN

Always brooding about this is driving you crazy; you never think about the things you should, and you insist on beating your head against a rock!

YERMA

A rock that is shameful—because it *is* a rock, when it should be a basket of flowers and sweet water!

JUAN

Being around you only makes me restless and uneasy. When there's no other choice, you should resign yourself.

YERMA

I came to this house so I wouldn't have to resign myself! When I'm in my coffin with my hands tied together and a cloth wrapped around my head to keep my mouth from falling open—that's when I'll resign myself!

JUAN

Then, what do you want to do?

YERMA

I want to drink water and there's no glass and no water! I want to walk up the hill, and I have no feet! I want to embroider my petticoats, and I can't find the thread!

JUAN

The truth is you're not a real woman, and you're trying to destroy a man who has no choice!

YERMA

I don't know who I am. Let go of me, let me unburden myself! I have never failed you!

JUAN

I don't like people pointing at me! That's why I want to see that door locked and everyone in her own house!

(FIRST SISTER-IN-LAW enters slowly and goes toward a cupboard)

YERMA

Talking to people is not a sin!

JUAN

But it can seem like one!

(The SECOND SISTER-IN-LAW enters and goes to the pitchers, from which she fills a water jug)

(Lowering his voice) I don't have the strength for all this. When people start a conversation, close your mouth and remember you're a married woman!

YERMA

(Amazed) Married!

JUAN

And that families have their honor, and honor is a burden all of them must bear!

(The SECOND SISTER-IN-LAW slowly exits with the water jug)

But inside our bloodstream it's dark and weak.

(The SISTER-IN-LAW exits with a tray. Her gait is almost processional. Pause)

Forgive me.

(YERMA looks at her husband; he raises his head and is held by her gaze)

Though, the way you are looking at me, I shouldn't say "Forgive me." I should force you, lock you up, because that's what a husband is for!

(The TWO SISTERS-IN-LAW *appear at the door)*

YERMA

I beg you not to talk! Let the matter rest!

(Pause)

JUAN

Let's eat!

(The TWO SISTERS-IN-LAW *exit)*

Did you hear me?

YERMA

(Sweetly) You eat with your sisters. I'm not hungry yet.

JUAN

As you wish. *(He exits)*

YERMA
(As if in a dream)
Oh, what a pasture of pain!
Oh, the gate barred against beauty!
I crave to carry a child, but the breeze
Offers dahlias made of the dreaming moon.
Deep in my flesh I have two warm springs,
Throbbing fountainheads of milk—
Two pulsing hoofbeats of a horse,
Which agitate the branches of my anguish.
O blind breasts under my clothing!
O doves without eyes, doves without whiteness!
The stinging pain of imprisoned blood
Nails hornets to the nape of my neck!
But surely you'll come, my love, my son!
As the sea gives salt, and the earth bears grain,
Our womb will swell with a tender child,
Like a cloud which brings the sweet, fresh rain.

(Looking toward the door) María, why do you pass my house in such a hurry?

MARIA

(Entering with a baby in her arms) When I have the baby with me, I do—since you always cry!

YERMA

That's true. *(She takes the baby and sits down)*

MARIA

It makes me sad that you are envious. *(She sits down)*

YERMA

I'm not envious—I'm deprived.

MARIA

Don't complain.

YERMA

How can I keep from complaining, when I see you and the other women in full bloom, and I see myself useless in the middle of so much beauty?

MARIA

But you have other things. If you'd listen to me, you could be happy.

YERMA

A country girl who doesn't bear children is as useless as a handful of thorns—even sinful! And so, I'm part of the refuse discarded by God's hand!

(MARIA reaches for the child)

Take him, he's happier with you! I suppose I don't have a mother's hands!

MARIA

Why do you say that?

YERMA

(Getting up) Because I'm sick of it! Because I'm sick of having them and not being able to use them for the right thing. Because I am hurt—hurt and completely degraded—watching how the wheat springs up, how the fountains never cease giving water, and how the sheep give birth to hundreds of lambs, and the dogs, and how it seems as if the whole countryside rises up to show me its young offspring, drowsily nursing, while I feel two blows of a hammer, here, where my baby's mouth should be!

MARIA

I don't like what you're saying!

YERMA

You women who have children, you can't understand those of us who don't! You stay fresh, ignorant—like people who swim in sweet water with no idea of what thirst is.

MARIA

I don't want to tell you what I always tell you.

YERMA

Each time I have more need, and less hope!

MARIA

How awful!

YERMA

I'll end up believing that I'm my own son. I often go down to feed the oxen—which I never used to do, because women don't—and when I walk through the dark shed, my footsteps sound to me like those of a man.

MARIA

We are all here for a reason.

YERMA

In spite of everything, he goes on wanting me. Now you see how I live!

MARIA

What about his sisters?

YERMA

I'll be dead and buried before I'll ever speak to them!

MARIA

What about your husband?

YERMA

The three of them are against me.

MARIA

What do they think?

YERMA

They imagine things. Like people with a guilty conscience. They think I could want another man, and don't realize that even if I did, in my family, honor comes first! They are stones in my path! But they don't know that if I want to, I can become a torrent of water and sweep them away!

(A SISTER *enters and then exits, carrying a loaf of bread)*

MARIA

Anyway, I think your husband still loves you.

YERMA

My husband gives me bread and board.

MARIA

What a hard time you're having, what a hard time! But remember the wounds of Our Lord.

(They are at the doorway)

YERMA

(Looking at the child) He's awake now.

MARIA

In a little while, he'll start to sing!

YERMA

The same eyes as you, you know that? Have you see them?
(Weeping) He has the same eyes that you have.

*(YERMA gently pushes MARIA, who leaves in silence. YERMA goes
toward the door through which her husband left)*

(The SECOND GIRL appears)

SECOND GIRL

Psst!

YERMA

(Turning) What?

SECOND GIRL

I waited for her to leave. My mother is expecting you.

YERMA

Is she alone?

SECOND GIRL

Two neighbors are with her.

YERMA

Tell them to wait a bit.

SECOND GIRL

But are you going? Aren't you afraid?

YERMA

I am going.

SECOND GIRL

Whatever you say!

YERMA

Have them wait for me, even if it's late!

(VICTOR enters)

VICTOR

Is Juan at home?

YERMA

Yes.

SECOND GIRL

(Conspiring) As I was saying, I'll bring the blouse later.

YERMA

Whenever you like.

(The GIRL leaves)

Sit down.

VICTOR

I'm fine this way.

YERMA

(Calling) Juan!

VICTOR

I've come to say goodbye.

(She trembles slightly, but recovers her composure)

YERMA

Are you going to live with your brothers?

VICTOR

That's what my father wants.

YERMA

He must be old now.

VICTOR

Yes, very old.

(Pause)

YERMA

A change of scenery will do you good.

VICTOR

All scenery is the same.

YERMA

No. I would go very far away.

VICTOR

It's all the same. The same sheep have the same wool.

YERMA

For men, yes; but women are another matter. I never heard a man who was eating say: "How good these apples are!" You go on your way without noticing the nice things. As for me, I can say I have hated the water from these wells!

VICTOR

It could be.

(The stage is in soft shadow)

YERMA

Victor.

VICTOR

Yes.

YERMA

Why are you leaving? Everybody here likes you.

VICTOR

I've behaved.

(Pause)

YERMA

You've behaved. One time, when you were a strong young shepherd, you carried me in your arms, don't you remember? You never know what's going to happen.

VICTOR

Everything changes.

YERMA

Some things don't change! There are things locked up behind the walls that can never change, because nobody hears them!

VICTOR

That's how it is.

(The SECOND SISTER-IN-LAW *appears and goes slowly toward the door, where she stands still, illuminated by the last light of afternoon)*

YERMA

But if they suddenly exploded, they would shake the world!

VICTOR

Nothing would be gained. The water in its channel, the flock in the fold, the moon in the sky, and a man with his plow!

YERMA

What a terrible shame not to be able to learn from the teachings of the old people!

(There is the long, melancholy sound made by a shepherd blowing on a conch shell)

VICTOR

The flocks.

JUAN

(Entering) Are you on your way now?

VICTOR

I want to get through the mountain pass before daybreak.

JUAN

Do I owe you anything?

VICTOR

No. You paid me well.

JUAN

(To YERMA*)* I bought his flocks.

YERMA

Yes?

VICTOR

(To YERMA*)* They're yours.

YERMA

I didn't know.

JUAN

(With satisfaction) It's true!

VICTOR

Your husband should see his fortune made!

YERMA

He who labors gets the fruit.

(The SISTER-IN-LAW *who is at the door goes inside)*

JUAN

We don't have enough room for so many sheep!

YERMA

(Somberly) There's so much land!

(Pause)

JUAN

We'll go together as far as the stream.

VICTOR

I wish great happiness for this house! *(He shakes* YERMA*'s hand)*

YERMA

May God hear you. Stay well!

*(*VICTOR *starts to leave, but after an imperceptible movement by*
YERMA, *he turns back)*

VICTOR

Did you say something?

YERMA

(Dramatically) I said, "Stay well!"

Thank you.

(They leave. YERMA *is left in anguish, looking at the hand which* VICTOR *shook. Then she quickly crosses to the left and picks up a shawl)*

SECOND GIRL
(Entering) Let's go! *(In silence, she covers* YERMA*'s head)*

YERMA
Let's go!

(They leave stealthily. The stage is almost dark. The FIRST SISTER-IN-LAW *enters with an oil lamp, which casts the only light on the stage. She goes to the edge of the stage, looking for* YERMA. *The shepherds' conch shells sound)*

FIRST SISTER-IN-LAW
(Softly) Yerma!

(The SECOND SISTER-IN-LAW *enters. They look at each other and then move toward the door)*

SECOND SISTER-IN-LAW
(Louder) Yerma!

FIRST SISTER-IN-LAW
(As she goes out the door, in an imperious voice) YERMA!

(We hear shepherds' horns and their dogs. The stage is extremely dark)

CURTAIN

ACT III

SCENE I

(The house of DOLORES THE CONJURER. *Day is breaking.* YERMA *enters with* DOLORES *and* TWO OLD WOMEN*)*

DOLORES

You were very brave!

FIRST OLD WOMAN

There's no force in the world like that of desire.

SECOND OLD WOMAN

But the cemetery was so dark!

DOLORES

I've said those prayers in the cemetery many times with women eager to have babies, and they were all afraid! All but you!

YERMA

I came for the result. I don't believe you're a dreadful woman.

DOLORES

I'm not! Let my tongue crawl with ants, like the mouths of the dead, if I have ever told a lie! The last time, I said the prayer with a beggar woman who'd been dry much longer than you, and her womb sweetened so beautifully she had two babies, down there by the river, because she didn't have time to get to the village, and she herself brought them in swaddling clothes for me to tend to.

YERMA

And she was able to walk here from the river?

DOLORES
She got here. With her shoes and her petticoats soaked with blood—but with her face shining!

YERMA
And nothing happened to her?

DOLORES
What could happen? God is God.

YERMA
Of course, God is God! Nothing could happen to her. Just pick up the babies and wash them in fresh water! Animals lick them, don't they? With my own child, that wouldn't disgust me. I have the notion that women who have just given birth are glowing inside, and that their babies sleep on top of them for hours and hours, listening to the stream of warm milk that goes on filling their breasts so they can suckle, so they can play until they don't want any more, until they pull their heads away. "Just a little bit more, my child . . ." And their faces and chests are covered with white drops!

DOLORES
Now you will have a child. I can assure you.

YERMA
I will have one because I must! Or I don't understand the world. Sometimes, when I'm sure that never, never . . . a wave of fire sweeps up from my feet, and makes everything seem empty. And men walking along the street, and bulls and stones, seem to me like things made of cotton. And I ask myself: "What are they there for?"

FIRST OLD WOMAN
It's all right for a married woman to want children, but if she doesn't have them, why this anxiety for them? What's important in this world is just to drift along with the years. I'm not crit-

icizing you. You saw how I helped with the praying. But what lush land do you hope to leave your son, or what good fortune, or what silver throne?

YERMA

I don't think about tomorrow, I think about today! You're old, and now you see everything like a book you've read before. I think I am thirsty, but I have no freedom! I want to hold my child in my arms so I can sleep peacefully! And listen carefully, and don't be frightened by what I say: even if I knew that one day my son was going to torture me, and hate me, and drag me through the streets by the hair, I would still rejoice at his birth! It's much better to cry over a man who is alive and stabs you with a knife than to cry over this phantom sitting on my heart, year after year!

FIRST OLD WOMAN

You're too young to listen to advice! But while you're waiting for the Grace of God, you should find shelter in your husband's love.

YERMA

Ay! You've put your finger into the deepest wound in my flesh!

DOLORES

Your husband is good.

YERMA

(She gets up) He is good. He is good! What of it? I wish he were bad! But no! He takes his sheep along their paths and counts his money at night. When he takes me, he is doing his duty, but his body feels as cold as a corpse! I have always been disgusted by hot-blooded women, but at that moment I would like to be a mountain of fire!

DOLORES

Yerma!

I'm not an unfaithful wife, but I know that children are conceived by a man and a woman. Oh, if only I could have them all by myself!

DOLORES

Think how your husband suffers, too.

YERMA

He doesn't suffer! The fact is, he doesn't want children.

FIRST OLD WOMAN

Don't say that!

YERMA

I can see it in his eyes, and since he doesn't want them, he doesn't give them to me. I don't love him, I don't love him, and yet he's my only salvation! For honor and for family! My only salvation!

FIRST OLD WOMAN

(Fearfully) Soon it will be dawn! You should go home.

DOLORES

Before you know it, the flocks will be coming out, and it's not good for you to be seen alone!

YERMA

I needed to get this off my chest. How many times do I repeat the prayers?

DOLORES

The prayer of the laurel twice, and at noon the prayer of Santa Ana. When you feel you're pregnant, bring me the bushel of wheat you promised me.

FIRST OLD WOMAN

Now it's beginning to grow light on top of the hills. Go!

Any minute, people will be opening their doors, so you'd better go around by the water ditch.

YERMA

(*Disheartened*) I don't know why I came.

DOLORES

Are you sorry?

YERMA

No!

DOLORES

(*Upset*) If you're afraid, I'll go with you as far as the corner.

FIRST OLD WOMAN

(*Uneasily*) It will be daylight by the time you get to your door.

(*Voices are heard*)

DOLORES

Be quiet!

(*They listen*)

FIRST OLD WOMAN

It's no one. God go with you!

(YERMA *goes toward the door, but at that moment a knock is heard. The three women stop still*)

DOLORES

Who is it?

JUAN'S VOICE

It's me!

Open it!

(DOLORES is unsure)

Are you going to open or not?

(Murmuring is heard. JUAN and the SISTERS-IN-LAW appear)

SECOND SISTER-IN-LAW

Here she is!

YERMA

Here I am!

JUAN

What are you doing in this place? If I could shout, I would rouse the whole village so they could see what's become of my family honor! But I have to choke it all back and keep quiet, because you are my wife.

YERMA

If I could, I would shout, too—so even the dead would rise up and see that I am cloaked in purity!

JUAN

No, not that! I can put up with anything but that! You deceive me, you confuse me, but I'm only a man who works the land and I can't compete with your cleverness!

DOLORES

Juan!

JUAN

Not a word out of any of you!

(Firmly) Your wife has done nothing wrong.

JUAN

She's been doing it since the very day of our wedding. Looking daggers at me, spending the nights on watch, lying at my side with her eyes open, and filling my pillows with her unhappy sighs!

YERMA

Shut your mouth!

JUAN

And I can't stand any more! You'd have to be made of bronze to put up with a woman at your side who wants to jab her fingers into your heart and goes out of her house at night— looking for what? Tell me! Looking for what? The streets are full of young studs. You don't go out on the streets to pick flowers!

YERMA

I won't let you say one more word! Not one more! You and your family think you're the only people who care about honor, and you don't know that my family has never had anything to hide. Come here! Come close to me and smell my clothing; come close! Let's see where you can find a smell that's not yours, that's not from your body! Stand me naked in the middle of the plaza and spit on me! Do what you like with me, since I'm your wife, but take care you don't put another man's name on my breast!

JUAN

It's not me who puts it there—you put it there with your behavior, and the town is beginning to talk! Beginning to talk! When I join a group of people, they all grow quiet. When I go to weigh the flour, they all grow quiet. And even at night, when

I wake up in the fields, it seems as if the branches of the trees grow quiet, too!

YERMA

Those evil winds that knock the wheat down—I don't know why they start. See for yourself if the wheat is good!

JUAN

Nor do I know what a woman is looking for, out of her house at all hours!

YERMA

(In an outburst, embracing her husband) I'm looking for you! I'm looking for you! It's you I look for, day and night, without finding any shade where I can rest! It's your blood and your help I want!

JUAN

Get away!

YERMA

Don't push me away—want *with* me!

JUAN

Stop it!

YERMA

See how alone I am! Like the moon trying to find herself in the sky. Look at me! *(She looks at him)*

JUAN

(Looking at her, and brusquely pushing her away) Leave me alone, once and for all!

DOLORES

Juan!

(YERMA *falls to the ground*)

YERMA

(Loudly) When I went out to pick my carnations I ran into the wall. *(She wails)* That is the wall where I have to smash my head to bits!

JUAN

Be quiet! Let's go!

DOLORES

My God!

YERMA

(Screaming) God damn my father for giving me his blood—the blood of the father of a hundred sons! God damn my blood that pounds on the walls looking for them!

JUAN

Be quiet, I said!

DOLORES

People are coming! Talk softly!

YERMA

I don't care! At least let my voice be free, now that I'm falling into the darkest part of the pit! *(She gets up)* Let my body send out just one beautiful thing, and let it fill the air.

(Voices are heard)

DOLORES

They're going to pass by here.

JUAN

Silence!

YERMA

Of course. Of course. Silence. Don't worry.

JUAN

Let's go! Quickly!

YERMA

All right! All right! And there's no use wringing my hands. Wanting something in your mind is one thing—

JUAN

Be quiet!

YERMA

(In a low voice) Wanting something in your head is one thing, but it's something else when your body—damn the body!— won't respond. This is my fate and I'm not going to fight against the tide. That's it! Let my lips be sealed! *(She leaves)*

FAST CURTAIN

SCENE 2

(On the grounds of a shrine, high in the mountains. Downstage, the wheels of a cart and some blankets form a crude tent where YERMA *sits.* WOMEN *enter, bringing offerings to the shrine. They are barefoot. In the group is the spirited* PAGAN OLD WOMAN *from Act I)*

SONG

I couldn't see you,
When you were single,
But now that you're married,
I will find you.
I'll strip you naked,
Wife and pilgrim,
When, in the dark,
The clock strikes twelve.

PAGAN OLD WOMAN

(Roguishly) Did you drink the holy water yet?

FIRST WOMAN

Yes.

PAGAN OLD WOMAN

And now we'll see about this one.

SECOND WOMAN

We believe in him.

PAGAN OLD WOMAN

You all come to ask the Saint to give you children, and the result is that each year more men come alone on this pilgrimage. What goes on here? *(She laughs)*

FIRST WOMAN

Why do you come here if you don't believe?

PAGAN OLD WOMAN

To watch. I love to watch! And to look after my son. Last year two men killed each other over one of these dried-up wives, and I want to keep an eye on him. And finally, I come because I feel like it!

FIRST WOMAN

May God forgive you!

(The WOMEN *exit)*

PAGAN OLD WOMAN

(Sarcastically, as she leaves) May he forgive you!

(MARIA and the FIRST GIRL *enter)*

FIRST GIRL

Has she come?

MARIA

There is her cart. I had a hard time getting them to come. For the past month, she hasn't been out of her chair. She frightens me! She has something in mind; I don't know what it is, but you can be sure it's nothing good!

FIRST GIRL

I came with my sister. She's been coming for eight years without results.

MARIA

You have children if you are meant to have them.

FIRST GIRL

That's what I say!

(There are voices offstage)

MARIA

I never liked this pilgrimage! Let's go to the threshing floor, that's where everyone is!

FIRST GIRL

Last year, when it got dark, some young men were grabbing my sister's breasts!

MARIA

For ten miles around, you hear nothing but filthy language!

FIRST GIRL

I saw more than forty barrels of wine in the back of the shrine!

MARIA

A river of men without women flows down these mountains!

(They exit. Offstage voices. YERMA *enters with six* WOMEN *who are going to the church. They are barefoot and carry spiral candles. Dusk begins to fall)*

FIRST WOMAN

Lord, let all the roses bloom,
Don't leave mine in the shade!

SECOND WOMAN

Upon your withered flesh
The yellow rose will bloom.

THIRD WOMAN

And in the womb of your servants,
The dark flame of the earth.

CHORUS OF WOMEN

Lord, let the roses bloom,
Don't leave mine in the shade!

(They kneel)

YERMA

Heaven is full of gardens
With roses of happiness,
And there among the roses
Is one miraculous rose.
It's like the light of morning;
An archangel guards it well,
With wings like enormous storm clouds,
And eyes like agonies.
And all around its petals,
Springs of sweet, warm milk
Frolic and bathe the faces
Of the tranquil stars.
Lord, open your rose
Upon my withered flesh!

(They get up)

SECOND WOMAN

Lord, cool with your hand
The burning coals of her cheek!

YERMA

Listen to the penitent
On your holy pilgrimage.
Open your rose in my flesh,
The rose with a thousand thorns.

CHORUS OF WOMEN

Lord, let the roses bloom,
Don't leave mine in the shade!

YERMA

Over my withered flesh,
One miraculous rose!

(They exit. Four YOUNG GIRLS *come running out from the left with long ribbons in their hands. From the right, three* OTHERS *with long ribbons, looking back over their shoulders. There is a crescendo of shouting and the sounds of cowbells and harness bells. On an upper level, the seven* YOUNG GIRLS *wave their ribbons toward the left. The racket increases, as two mummers enter, one as a* MALE, *the other as a* FEMALE. *They wear large folk masks. The* MALE *clutches the horn of a bull in his hand. They are not grotesque in any way, but are of great beauty and pure earthiness. The* FEMALE *shakes a necklace of large jingle bells. Upstage, a crowd of* PEOPLE *shout and cheer the* DANCERS *on. Night has fallen)*

CHILDREN

The devil and his wife! The devil and his wife!

FEMALE

In the river in the mountains,
The despondent wife was bathing.
Up along her naked body,
Tiny water snails were climbing.
The sand along the river edge,
The breeze of early morning,
Set her laughter all afire,
Made her shoulders tremble,

Oh, she was naked, laughing,
The maiden in the water!

BOY

Oh, how she was moaning!

FIRST MAN

Oh, thirsty for love!
Dry, in the wind and the water!

SECOND MAN

Who is the one you're awaiting?

FIRST MAN

Who is the one you watch for?

SECOND MAN

Oh, with your womb that is dry,
And with your color fading!

FEMALE

When night has come, I'll say it;
When night has come, transparent,
When night has come to the ritual,
I'll tear my petticoats open!

BOY

And night was falling quickly.
Oh, how the night was falling!
See how the darkness gathers
At the waterfall on the mountain.

(Guitars begin to play)

MALE
(Rising and shaking the horn)
Oh, how white she is,

The despondent wife!
Oh, how she moans in the branches!
Later, she will be
A poppy, a carnation—
Later, when the male
Opens up his cape.
                    (He comes nearer)
If you come to the ritual,
Pray your womb will open.
Don't put on a veil of mourning,
Wear your softest, finest linen.
Go alone behind the walls
Where the fig trees have been hidden.
Lie beneath my earthen body
Till the first white sigh of dawn.
Oh, how she is glowing!
Oh, how she was glowing!
Oh, how the wife is swaying!

FEMALE

Oh, how love endows her
With garlands and with crowns;
And darts of molten gold
Penetrate her breast!

MALE

Seven times she moaned
And nine times she rose
And fifteen times the jasmine
Fused with the orange.

THIRD MAN

Strike her with the horn!

SECOND MAN

Again, the rose, the dance!

FIRST MAN

Oh, how the wife is swaying!

MALE

In this ritual,
The male takes command.
Married men are bulls:
The male takes command.
Now, bestow the wreath—
The pilgrim girls are flowers
For the man who wins them!

BOY

Strike her with the wind!

SECOND MAN

Strike her with the wreath!

MALE

Come and see the glow
Of the wife who was bathing!

FIRST MAN

She bends like a reed.

BOY

She fades like a flower.

MEN

Let the little girls leave!

MALE

Let them burn: the dance
And the glowing body
Of the innocent wife!

(They are dancing off, smiling, to the sound of hand claps. They sing)

Heaven is full of gardens,
With roses of happiness,
And there among the roses
Is one miraculous rose.

(Two YOUNG GIRLS *go by again, shouting. The cheerful* OLD WOMAN *enters)*

OLD WOMAN

Let's see if you let us sleep later on! But later on, it will be her turn!

*(*YERMA *enters)*

You!

*(*YERMA *is downcast, and does not speak)*

Tell me, why did you come?

YERMA

I don't know.

OLD WOMAN

You're not convinced? Where's your husband?

*(*YERMA *shows signs of exhaustion and of being overcome by her obsession)*

YERMA

He's over there.

OLD WOMAN

What is he doing?

YERMA

Drinking. *(She pauses, then raises hands to her forehead)* Ay!

OLD WOMAN

"Ay!" "Ay!" Less "Ay!" and more spirit! I couldn't tell you anything before, but now I can.

YERMA

What are you going to tell me that I don't already know?

OLD WOMAN

Something that can't be kept quiet anymore. Something they are shouting from the rooftops! It's your husband's fault! Do you hear? They can cut off my hands! Neither his father nor his grandfather nor his great-grandfather behaved like a breed of real men. Heaven and earth had to come together for them to have a son! They're put together with spit! Not like your people. You have brothers and cousins for a hundred miles around! See what a curse has fallen upon your beauty!

YERMA

A curse! A pool of poison over the wheat!

OLD WOMAN

But you have feet: you can walk out of your house!

YERMA

Walk out?

OLD WOMAN

When I saw you at the pilgrimage, my heart turned over! Women come here to find other men. And the Saint performs the miracle! My son is sitting behind the shrine waiting for you. My house needs a woman! Go with him and the three of us will live together. My son has good blood in his veins! Like me! If you come to my house, it still smells like cradles! The ashes of your bedsheets will be bread and salt for your children. Go on! Don't worry about people. And as for your husband, there are enough brave hearts and sharp tools in my house to keep him from even crossing the street!

YERMA

Be quiet, be quiet, it's not that! I'd never do that! I can't go out looking. Do you think that I could have another man? What about my honor? You can't turn back the tide, or have a full moon come out at midday! Go away! I'll continue on the road I have chosen. Did you really think that I could turn to another man? That I'm going to beg like a slave for what belongs to me? Know who I am, so that you will never speak to me again! I am not looking for anyone.

OLD WOMAN

When you're thirsty, you're grateful for water.

YERMA

I'm like a parched field big enough to hold a thousand teams of oxen plowing, and what you give me is a little glass of water from the well! Mine is pain that is no longer of my flesh!

OLD WOMAN

(Loud) Then go on this way. It's what you want! Like thistles in the wasteland—prickly, barren!

YERMA

(Loud) Barren, yes, I already know it! Barren! It's not necessary to rub my mouth in it! Don't amuse yourself like little children do with a dying animal! Ever since I got married, I've been turning that word over in my mind, but it's the first time I've heard it, the first time it's been said to my face! The first time I know that it's true!

OLD WOMAN

I have no pity for you, none! I will look for another woman for my son!

(She goes. A large chorus of pilgrims is singing in the distance. YERMA *goes toward the cart, and her husband appears from behind it)*

YERMA

You were there?

JUAN

I was.

YERMA

Listening?

JUAN

Listening.

YERMA

And you heard?

JUAN

Yes.

YERMA

What of it! Leave me alone and go join the singers! *(She sits down in the tent)*

JUAN

It's also time for me to speak.

YERMA

Speak!

JUAN

And complain.

YERMA

About what?

JUAN

I have a bitterness in my throat.

YERMA

And I, in my bones!

JUAN

I can no longer put up with this constant grieving over obscure things, unreal things made of thin air.

YERMA

(Dramatically) Unreal, you call it? Thin air, you call it?

JUAN

Over things that have not happened and that neither you nor I can control.

YERMA

(Violently) Go on! Go on!

JUAN

Over things I don't care about! Do you hear? That I don't care about! I finally have to tell you! All I care about is what I can hold in my hands. What I can see with my eyes!

YERMA

(Falling to her knees in desperation) That's it, that's it! That's what I wanted to hear from your lips! You can't see the truth when it's inside you, but how huge it is, and how it screams, when it comes out and raises its arms! You don't care! At last I have heard it!

JUAN

(Coming near her) Tell yourself it had to turn out this way. Listen to me! *(He puts his arms around her to lift her to her feet)* Many women would be happy living the life you do. Life is sweeter without children! I'm happy not having them. We're not to blame in any way!

YERMA

Then what were you looking for in me?

JUAN

For you yourself!

YERMA

(With excitement) That's it! You were looking for a house, peace and quiet, and a wife! But nothing more. Is it true, what I'm saying?

JUAN

It's true! Like everyone.

YERMA

What about the rest? What about your son?

JUAN

(Fiercely) Didn't you hear that I don't care? Don't ask me anymore! I'll have to shout it in your ear for you to understand! Now let's see if once and for all you can live in peace!

YERMA

And you never considered having a son, when you saw how much I wanted one?

JUAN

Never!

(They are both on the ground)

YERMA

And I have no hope?

JUAN

No.

YERMA

Nor you?

JUAN

Nor me either. Accept it!

Barren!

JUAN

And we shall live in peace. Both of us, quietly, with pleasure.
Embrace me! *(He embraces her)*

YERMA

What are you after?

JUAN

You are what I'm after! In the moonlight, you are beautiful!

YERMA

You pursue me as if I were a dove you want to devour!

JUAN

Kiss me—like this!

YERMA

Never! Never!

*(YERMA cries out and clutches her husband by the throat. He falls
back. She chokes him until she kills him. The pilgrims' chorus begins)*

YERMA

Barren. Barren, but sure. Now I know it for certain. And alone.

(She stands up. People begin to gather)

I will sleep without suddenly waking up to see if my blood is
proclaiming other, new blood. With my body dry forever. What
do you want to know? Don't come near me, for I have killed
my son! I myself have killed my son!

(A group gathers and stays upstage. We hear the pilgrims' chorus)

CURTAIN

THE HOUSE OF

BERNARDA ALBA

A DRAMA OF WOMEN

IN THE VILLAGES

OF SPAIN

Cast of Characters

BERNARDA, *age 60*

MARIA JOSEFA *(Bernarda's mother), age 80*

ANGUSTIAS *(Bernarda's daughter), age 39*

MAGDALENA *(Bernarda's daughter), age 30*

AMELIA *(Bernarda's daughter), age 27*

MARTIRIO *(Bernarda's daughter), age 24*

ADELA *(Bernarda's daughter), age 20*

MAID, *age 50*

PONCIA *(maid), age 60*

PRUDENCIA, *age 50*

BEGGAR WOMAN *with her* LITTLE GIRL

WOMEN MOURNERS:

FIRST WOMAN

SECOND WOMAN

THIRD WOMAN

FOURTH WOMAN

GIRL

*The poet advises that these three acts
are intended as a photographic documentary.*

ACT I

(A very white inner room in BERNARDA's *house. Thick walls. Arched doorways with jute curtains trimmed with black beads and ruffles. Rush-bottom chairs. Pictures of nymphs or legendary kings in improbable landscapes. It is summer. A great shady silence envelops the stage. When the curtain rises, the stage is empty. Church bells are tolling. The* MAID *enters)*

MAID

My head is bursting with those tolling bells.

PONCIA

(Entering, eating bread and sausage) They've been mumbling away for more than two hours now. Priests have come from every town. The church looks beautiful! Magdalena fainted during the first response.

MAID

She's the one who's going to be the loneliest.

PONCIA

She's the only one her father loved. Oh, thank God we're alone for a moment! I came back here to eat.

MAID

If Bernarda should see you . . . !

PONCIA

Since she doesn't eat, she'd like it if we all starved. Bossy! Tyrant! But she'll be the loser—I've opened her jar of sausages.

MAID

(Sadly, with longing) Poncia, why don't you give me some for my little girl?

PONCIA

Come take a handful of garbanzos, too. Today she won't notice.

VOICE

(From within) Bernarda!

PONCIA

The old lady. Is she locked up tight?

MAID

With two turns of the key.

PONCIA

You should fasten the bolt, too. She has fingers like five skeleton keys!

VOICE

Bernarda!

PONCIA

(Calling out) She's coming! *(To the* MAID*)* Scrub everything clean. If Bernarda doesn't see things shine, she'll tear out the little hair I have left!

MAID

What a woman!

PONCIA

She tyrannizes everyone around her. She could sit on your heart and watch you die for a whole year without taking that cold smile off her damn face! Scrub! Scrub those tiles!

MAID

My hands are bleeding from all this scrubbing.

PONCIA

She—the most immaculate—the most decent. She—the most superior! Her poor husband has earned a good rest.

(The bells stop tolling)

MAID

Did all the relatives come?

PONCIA

Hers did. His people hate her. They just came to see him dead, make the sign of the cross, and get out.

MAID

Are there enough chairs?

PONCIA

More than enough. Let them sit on the floor! Since Bernarda's father died, people haven't been back to this house. She doesn't want them to see her in her domain. Damn her!

MAID

She's been good to you.

PONCIA

Thirty years, washing her sheets. Thirty years, eating her leftovers. Nights watching over her when she coughs. Entire days peering through cracks, to spy on the neighbors and bring her the gossip. A life with no secrets from each other. And yet—damn her! May she have a horrible pain—like nails stuck in her eyes!

MAID

Poncia!

PONCIA

But I'm a good dog: I bark when I'm told to, and I snap at beggars' heels when she sets me on them. My sons work in her fields, and they're both married now, but someday I'll be sick of it.

And on that day . . . ?

PONCIA

On that day I'll lock myself in a room with her and spit at her for a whole year! "For this, Bernarda!" "And for that!" "And for the other!" Until she's like a lizard that children have smashed to pieces. That's what she is! And so is her whole family. I certainly don't envy the way she lives. She has five girls on her hands, five ugly daughters, but except for Augustias, the oldest—who is her first husband's child and has some money— the rest: lots of fine lace, lots of linen shifts, but bread and grapes is all they will inherit!

MAID

I would like to have what they have.

PONCIA

What you and I have is our hands and a hole to be buried in when we die.

MAID

That's all the land they give to us who have nothing!

PONCIA

(At the cupboard) This crystal has some spots on it.

MAID

Neither soap nor flannel will get them off.

(The bells ring)

PONCIA

The last prayer—I'm going over to listen. I love the way the priest sings! In the Pater Noster his voice rose higher and higher—like a water pitcher being filled little by little. Of course, at the end it cracked, but it's glorious to hear him. Even so, there's no one like old Earsplitter, the sacristan. He sang at the

Mass for my mother, may she rest in peace. The walls trembled, and when he sang the "Amen," it was as if a wolf had come into the church. *(Imitating him)* AME-E-EN!" *(She starts to cough)*

MAID

You'll pulverize your windpipe!

PONCIA

I'd rather pulverize something else! *(She exits, laughing)*

(The MAID scrubs. The bells ring)

MAID

(Imitating the bells) Ding ding dong! Ding ding dong! May God forgive him.

BEGGAR WOMAN

(Coming in with a little girl) Blessed be God!

MAID

Ding ding dong! Ding ding dong! May he wait many years for us! Ding ding dong!

BEGGAR WOMAN

(Loud, with a certain irritation) Blessed be God!

MAID

(Irritated) Forever!

BEGGAR WOMAN

I've come for the leftovers.

(The bells stop ringing)

MAID

You can get to the street right through that door. Today's leftovers are for me!

BEGGAR WOMAN

But you have someone to support you. My daughter and I are alone!

MAID

Dogs are alone too, and they get by.

BEGGAR WOMAN

They always give them to me.

MAID

Get out of here! Who said you could come in? Now you've tracked up my floor.

(They exit. The MAID *continues scrubbing)*

Floors polished with oil; cupboards, pedestals, steel beds. It's a bitter thing to swallow when you live in a mud hut with one plate and one spoon. I only hope someday not one of us will be left to tell about it.

(The bells start ringing again)

Yes, yes, toll away! Bring in the coffin with its gold trim and the silk towels to carry it with. In the end you will be the same as me. Rot away, Antonio María Benavides, stiff in your wool suit and your high boots! Rot away! Never again will you lift up my skirts behind the back corral!

(From the rear, women mourners begin to enter, two by two. They wear black skirts and shawls and carry black fans. They enter slowly, until they fill the stage. The MAID *breaks into a wail)*

Oh, Antonio María Benavides, you'll never again see these walls or eat the bread of this house! Of those who served you, I loved you the most! *(She is tearing her hair)* Must I go on living after you have gone? Must I go on living?

(As the two hundred women mourners finish coming in, BERNARDA ALBA *and her five daughters appear.* BERNARDA *is leaning on a cane)*

BERNARDA

(To the MAID*)* Silence!

MAID

(Crying) Bernarda!

BERNARDA

Less screaming and more work! You should have seen to it everything was cleaner to receive the mourners. Get out! This is not where you belong.

(The MAID *leaves, weeping)*

The poor are like animals; they seem to be made of other substances.

FIRST WOMAN

Poor people have their sorrows, too.

BERNARDA

But they forget them, once there's a plate of garbanzos in front of them!

GIRL

(Timidly) You must eat to live.

BERNARDA

At your age, one does not speak in front of one's elders.

FIRST WOMAN

Be quiet, child!

BERNARDA

I have never let anyone lecture me. Sit down.

(They sit. Pause)

Magdalena, don't cry! If you want to cry, crawl under the bed. Did you hear me?

SECOND WOMAN

(To BERNARDA*)* Have you begun to thresh your wheat?

BERNARDA

Yesterday.

THIRD WOMAN

The sun beats down like lead.

FIRST WOMAN

I haven't known it to be this hot in years.

(Pause. They all fan themselves)

BERNARDA

Is the lemonade ready?

PONCIA

Yes, Bernarda. *(She enters with a large tray full of small white cups, which she passes around)*

BERNARDA

Give some to the men.

PONCIA

They're having some on the patio.

BERNARDA

Have them leave the way they came in. I don't want them coming through here.

GIRL

(*To* ANGUSTIAS) Pepe el Romano was with the men at the funeral.

ANGUSTIAS

He was there.

BERNARDA

His mother was there. She saw his mother. Neither she nor I saw Pepe.

GIRL

I thought I saw him.

BERNARDA

The one who *was* there was that widower from Darajalí. Standing very close to your aunt. All of us saw him.

SECOND WOMAN

(*Aside, in a low voice*) Wicked! More than wicked!

THIRD WOMAN

(*Also in a low voice*) A tongue like a knife!

BERNARDA

In church, women should look at no man but the priest, and at him only because he's wearing skirts. Whoever turns her head is on the prowl for a man.

FIRST WOMAN

(*In a low voice*) Dried-up old lizard!

PONCIA

(*Muttering*) Twisted vine—reaching for the heat of a man!

BERNARDA

(*Striking the floor with her cane*) Blessed be God!

ALL

(Crossing themselves) Forever blessed and holy.

BERNARDA

Rest in peace, with the Souls of the Departed
Watching over you.

ALL

Rest in peace!

BERNARDA

With Saint Michael the Archangel
And his sword of justice.

ALL

Rest in peace!

BERNARDA

With the key that opens all
And the hand that closes all.

ALL

Rest in peace!

BERNARDA

With all the blessed saints
And the little lights of the fields.

ALL

Rest in peace!

BERNARDA

With our holy charity
And the souls from land and sea.

ALL

Rest in peace!

BERNARDA

Grant repose to your servant Antonio María Benavides, and give him the crown of your sacred glory.

ALL

Amen!

BERNARDA

(Getting to her feet and singing) Requiem aeternam dona eis, Domine.

ALL

(Standing and singing in the Gregorian mode) Et lux perpetua luceat eis. (They cross themselves)

FIRST WOMAN

Good health—to pray for his soul.

(They are filing out)

THIRD WOMAN

You'll never go without a hot loaf of bread.

SECOND WOMAN

Or shelter for your daughters.

(They all file past BERNARDA and leave. ANGUSTIAS exits through the patio door)

FOURTH WOMAN

May you continue to reap the profits of your married life.

PONCIA

(Entering with a money bag) The men left this bag of money for prayers.

BERNARDA

Thank them, and pour them a glass of brandy.

GIRL

(To MAGDALENA*)* Magdalena . . .

BERNARDA

(To MAGDALENA, *who is starting to cry) Sssh! (She bangs her cane. To the guests, who have all left)* Go back to your cares and criticize everything you've seen! I hope many years go by before you cross my threshold again!

PONCIA

You have nothing to complain about. The whole town came!

BERNARDA

Yes—to fill my house with the sweat of their underclothes and the poison of their tongues!

AMELIA

Mother, don't talk like that!

BERNARDA

That's the way you must talk in this damned town without a river, this town of wells! Where you always drink the water fearing that it's poisoned!

PONCIA

Look what they have done to the floor!

BERNARDA

You would think a herd of goats had walked on it!

*(*PONCIA *scrubs the floor)*

Adela, give me a fan.

ADELA

Here you are. *(She gives her a round fan decorated with red and green flowers)*

BERNARDA

(Hurling the fan to the floor) Is this the fan you give to a widow? Give me a black one, and learn to respect your father's memory!

MARTIRIO

Take mine.

BERNARDA

What about you?

MARTIRIO

I don't feel warm.

BERNARDA

Well, look for another—you're going to need one. During our eight years of mourning, no wind from the street will enter this house! Pretend we have sealed up the doors and windows with bricks. That was how it was in my father's house, and in my grandfather's house. In the meantime, you can begin to embroider your trousseaus. I have twenty bolts of linen in the chest from which you can cut sheets. Magdalena can embroider them.

MAGDALENA

It's all the same to me.

ADELA

(Acidly) If you don't want to embroider them, they'll go without embroidering. That way yours will stand out.

MAGDALENA

Neither mine nor yours. I know I'm not going to get married. I'd rather carry sacks to the mill. Anything but sit in this dark room, day after day!

BERNARDA

That's what it means to be a woman.

MAGDALENA

To hell with being a woman!

BERNARDA

Here you do what I tell you to do! You can't run to your father
with your stories anymore. A needle and thread for females; a
mule and a whip for males. That's how it is for people born
with means.

(ADELA exits)

VOICE

Bernarda! Let me out!

BERNARDA

(In a loud voice) Let her out now!

(The MAID enters)

MAID

I could barely hold her. Your mother is eighty years old, but
she's as strong as an oak.

BERNARDA

She takes after my grandfather. He was just the same.

MAID

Several times during the funeral, I had to cover her mouth with
an empty sack, because she wanted to call out to you, to give
her at least some dishwater to drink, and dog meat. That's what
she says you give her.

MARTIRIO

She's up to no good.

BERNARDA

(To the MAID) She can let off steam out in the patio.

MAID

She took her rings and the amethyst earrings out of her trunk.
She put them on and told me she wants to get married.

(The daughters laugh)

BERNARDA

Go with her, and be sure she doesn't go near the well.

MAID

Don't worry, she won't throw herself in!

BERNARDA

It's not that. Out there, the neighbors can see her from their
window.

(The MAID exits)

MARTIRIO

We're going to change our clothes.

BERNARDA

Very well, but don't take the kerchief off your head.

(ADELA enters)

Where is Angustias?

ADELA

(Pointedly) I saw her peering through a crack in the front door.
The men had just left.

BERNARDA

And you, why did you go to the door, too?

ADELA

I went to see if the hens had laid.

BERNARDA

But the men must have left already.

ADELA

(Pointedly) A group of them were still standing around outside.

BERNARDA

(Furious) Angustias! Angustias!

ANGUSTIAS

(As she enters) What do you want?

BERNARDA

What were you looking at? At whom?

ANGUSTIAS

At no one.

BERNARDA

Is it proper for a woman of your class to go chasing after a man on the day of her father's Funeral Mass? Answer me! Who were you looking at?

(Pause)

ANGUSTIAS

Me?

BERNARDA

You!

ANGUSTIAS

At no one.

BERNARDA

(Advancing on her with her cane) You weakling! You're sickening! (She strikes her)

PONCIA

(Running to her) Bernarda, calm down! (She holds on to her)

(ANGUSTIAS is crying)

BERNARDA

Get out of here! All of you!

(They leave)

PONCIA

She did it without thinking what she was doing—which was clearly wrong. It seemed strange to me to see her sneaking off toward the patio. And then she stood at the window, listening to the men's conversation—which, as always, was not fit to hear.

BERNARDA

That's why they come to funerals. (With curiosity) What were they talking about?

PONCIA

They were talking about Paca la Roseta. Last night they tied her husband up in a stall, threw her over the back of a horse, and carried her off to the top of the olive grove.

BERNARDA

What about her?

PONCIA

Her? She agreed to it. They say she rode with her breasts hanging out, and Maximiliano held her as if he were playing a guitar. How horrible!

BERNARDA

Then what happened?

PONCIA

What was bound to happen. It was dawn when they got back.
Paca la Roseta had her hair undone and was wearing a crown
of flowers on her head.

BERNARDA

She's the only loose woman we have in this town.

PONCIA

Because she's not from here. She's from far away. And the men
who went with her are the sons of strangers, too. The men
around here wouldn't dare do that.

BERNARDA

No. But they like to watch it and talk about it, and lick their
fingers about what goes on.

PONCIA

They said a lot more things.

BERNARDA

(Glancing from side to side with a certain fear) What?

PONCIA

I'm embarrassed to talk about them.

BERNARDA

And my daughter heard?

PONCIA

Of course!

BERNARDA

That one takes after her aunts. Soft and slippery—making sheep's
eyes at any little barber who flattered them! How one must suffer
and struggle to get people to behave decently and not like
savages!

Your daughters are old enough to get married now. They give you little enough trouble. Angustias must be well over thirty by now.

BERNARDA

Thirty-nine, to be exact.

PONCIA

Imagine! And she's never had a suitor.

BERNARDA

(Furious) None of them has had a suitor—nor needs one! They can get by very well.

PONCIA

I didn't mean to offend you.

BERNARDA

For a hundred miles around, no one can measure up to them. The men here are not of their class. What would you have me do—turn them over to some field hand?

PONCIA

You should have gone to some other town.

BERNARDA

Of course—to sell them!

PONCIA

No, Bernarda, to change . . . Of course, in other places, *they* would be the poor ones.

BERNARDA

Hold that vicious tongue!

PONCIA

No one can talk to you. Can we or can we not be honest with each other?

BERNARDA

We cannot. You are my servant, and I pay you. Nothing more!

MAID

(Entering) Don Arturo is here. He's come to discuss the will.

BERNARDA

Get busy! *(To the MAID)* You start scrubbing the patio. *(To PONCIA)* And you start putting away all the clothes of the deceased in the big chest.

PONCIA

We could give some things away.

BERNARDA

Nothing, not one button! Not even the handkerchief we used to cover his face!

(BERNARDA leaves slowly, leaning on her cane, with a final look at the servants. Then the MAID exits. AMELIA and MARTIRIO enter)

AMELIA

Have you taken your medicine?

MARTIRIO

For all the good it's going to do me!

AMELIA

But you *have* taken it.

MARTIRIO

I do things I have no faith in, but I do them like clockwork.

AMELIA

You seem livelier since the new doctor arrived.

MARTIRIO

I feel the same.

AMELIA

Did you notice? Adelaida wasn't at the funeral.

MARTIRIO

I knew she wouldn't be. Her fiancé won't let her go out, not even to the front door. She used to be full of fun; now she doesn't even powder her face!

AMELIA

Nowadays, you don't know whether it's better to get engaged or not.

MARTIRIO

It's all the same.

AMELIA

The problem is, we are always being criticized—they won't let us enjoy life. Adelaida must have had a terrible time.

MARTIRIO

She's afraid of Mother. She's the only one who knows the true story of her father and how he got his land. Every time she comes here, Mother needles her about it. Her father killed his first wife's husband in Cuba so he could marry her himself. Then, here, he deserted her and ran off with another woman, who had a daughter. And then he had an affair with this girl, Adelaida's mother, and he married her after his second wife went mad and died.

AMELIA

That despicable man, why isn't he in prison?

MARTIRIO

Because men cover up for each other on this kind of thing, and no one dares to make accusations.

AMELIA

But Adelaida is not to blame for that.

MARTIRIO

No. But things have a way of repeating themselves. And I see how it all follows a terrible pattern. And she'll suffer the same fate as her mother and her grandmother—the two wives of the man who fathered her.

AMELIA

What an awful thing!

MARTIRIO

It's better never to lay eyes on a man. Since I was a child, I've been afraid of them. I used to see them in the corral, yoking the oxen and loading the sacks of wheat, with loud voices and clumsy feet, and I was always afraid of growing up, for fear of suddenly finding myself in their clutches. God made me weak and ugly, and set them forever apart from me.

AMELIA

Don't say that! Enrique Humanas was after you and he used to like you.

MARTIRIO

The things people make up! One time I stood at the window in my nightgown until daylight because his field hand's daughter told me he was going to come, and he didn't. It was all just talk. Then he married someone with more money than me.

AMELIA

And ugly as the devil.

MARTIRIO

What do they care about ugliness? All they care about is land,
oxen, and a meek little dog to cook for them.

(AMELIA *sighs*. MAGDALENA *enters*)

MAGDALENA

What are you doing?

MARTIRIO

I'm just here.

AMELIA

And you?

MAGDALENA

I've been going through the storage rooms. To stretch my legs.
To see the pictures Grandmother embroidered on canvas—the
little wool dog, the black man wrestling with the lion—that we
liked so much when we were children. Those were happier times!
A wedding lasted ten days and wagging tongues were not the
fashion. Today there's more finesse, brides wear white veils like
in the big cities, and we drink bottled wine. But we rot away
inside about what people will say.

MARTIRIO

God knows what went on then!

AMELIA

(*To* MAGDALENA) One of your shoelaces is untied.

MAGDALENA

What difference does it make!

AMELIA

You'll step on it and you'll fall.

MAGDALENA

One less.

MARTIRIO

Where's Adela?

MAGDALENA

Ah! She put on the green dress she made to wear on her birthday; she went out to the corral and began to shout, "Chickens! Chickens, look at me!" I had to laugh.

AMELIA

If Mother had seen her!

MAGDALENA

Poor little thing! She's the youngest of us, and she has dreams. I would give anything to see her happy.

(Pause. ANGUSTIAS *crosses the stage, carrying some towels)*

ANGUSTIAS

What time is it?

MAGDALENA

It must be twelve by now.

ANGUSTIAS

So late?

AMELIA

It's just about to strike.

*(*ANGUSTIAS *exits)*

MAGDALENA

(Knowingly) Do you know about it yet? *(Indicating* ANGUSTIAS*)*

AMELIA

No.

MAGDALENA

Come on!

MARTIRIO

I don't know what you're referring to.

MAGDALENA

You two know more about it than I do. You always have your heads together like two little sheep, but you never confide in anyone else. About Pepe el Romano.

MARTIRIO

Ah!

MAGDALENA

(Mimicking her) Ah! They are already talking about it in town. Pepe el Romano wants to marry Angustias. He was circling the house last night, and I think he'll send someone to ask for her hand soon.

MARTIRIO

I'm glad. He's a good man.

AMELIA

Me, too. Angustias has good qualities.

MAGDALENA

Neither one of you is glad!

MARTIRIO

Magdalena! Really!

MAGDALENA

If he wanted Angustias for herself, Angustias as a woman, I would be glad. But he wants her money. Even though Angustias is our sister, in this family we know she's old, in poor health, and has always had the least to offer of any of us. After all, if she looked like a scarecrow when she was twenty, what can she look like now that she's forty?

MARTIRIO

Don't talk that way. Luck comes to the one who least expects it.

AMELIA

After all, she is telling the truth! Angustias has all her father's money. She is the only rich one in the house. That's why, now that our father is dead and the estate is being settled, they're coming after her.

MAGDALENA

Pepe el Romano is twenty-five years old, and the best-looking man around. It would be natural for him to be interested in you, Amelia, or in our Adela, who is twenty years old, but not to come looking for the gloomiest person in this house—a woman who talks through her nose, like her father did!

MARTIRIO

Maybe he likes that!

MAGDALENA

I never could stand your hypocrisy!

MARTIRIO

God help us!

(ADELA *enters*)

MAGDALENA

Have the chickens seen you yet?

ADELA

And what would you like me to do?

AMELIA

If Mother sees you, she'll drag you out by the hair.

ADELA

I had such dreams about this dress. I planned to wear it the day we were going out to eat watermelons down by the waterwheel. There wouldn't have been another like it!

MARTIRIO

It's a lovely dress.

ADELA

And it suits me very well. It's the best one Magdalena has ever made.

MAGDALENA

What did the chickens say?

ADELA

They made me a gift of a few fleas that bit my legs.

(They laugh)

MARTIRIO

What she could do is dye it black.

MAGDALENA

The best thing she could do is give it to Angustias to wear when she marries Pepe el Romano.

ADELA

(With restrained emotion) But Pepe el Romano . . . !

AMELIA

Haven't you heard?

ADELA

No.

MAGDALENA
Well, now you know!

ADELA
But that's not possible!

MAGDALENA
Money makes everything possible!

ADELA
Is that why she went out after the funeral and was looking through the door? *(She pauses)* And that man has the nerve to . . .

MAGDALENA
He has the nerve to do anything. *(Pause)*

MARTIRIO
What are you thinking, Adela?

ADELA
I'm thinking that this period of mourning has caught me at the worst possible time.

MAGDALENA
You'll soon get used to it.

ADELA
(Bursting into angry tears) I will not get used to it! I don't want to be locked up! I don't want my body to dry up like yours! I don't want to waste away and grow old in these rooms. To-morrow, I'll put on my green dress and go walking down the street. I want to get out!

(The MAID *enters)*

MAGDALENA
(With authority) Adela!

MAID

The poor thing! How she misses her father . . . *(She exits)*

MARTIRIO

Be quiet!

AMELIA

What goes for one goes for all!

(ADELA calms down)

MAGDALENA

The maid almost heard you.

(The MAID enters)

MAID

Pepe el Romano is coming down the street.

MAGDALENA

Let's go watch!

(AMELIA, MARTIRIO, and MAGDALENA run off quickly)

MAID

(To ADELA) You're not going?

ADELA

I don't care.

MAID

Since he'll be coming around the corner, you can see him better
from the window in your room.

*(The MAID exits. ADELA hesitates for a moment. Then she, too,
rushes off toward her room. BERNARDA and PONCIA enter)*

BERNARDA

That damned will!

PONCIA

What a lot of money was left to Angustias!

BERNARDA

Yes.

PONCIA

And to the others, so much less!

BERNARDA

You've said that to me three times now, and I didn't choose to answer you. So much less, a lot less—don't remind me of it again!

(ANGUSTIAS *enters. Her face is heavily powdered*)

Angustias!

ANGUSTIAS

Mother.

BERNARDA

Have you dared to powder your face? Have you dared even to *wash* your face, on the day of your father's death?

ANGUSTIAS

He was not my father! Mine died sometime ago. Don't you remember him any more?

BERNARDA

You owe more to that man, the father of your sisters, than you do to your own. Thanks to that man, your future is assured.

ANGUSTIAS

We'll see about that!

BERNARDA

If only out of decency. Out of respect!

ANGUSTIAS

Mother, let me go!

BERNARDA

Go? After you've taken that powder off your face! Weakling! Hussy! You're the image of your aunts! *(Furiously, she removes the powder from* ANGUSTIAS*'s face with her handerchief)* Now get out!

PONCIA

Bernarda, don't be so hard on her!

BERNARDA

My mother may have gone mad, but I am in control of myself. I know exactly what I'm doing.

(The other daughters enter)

MAGDALENA

What is going on?

BERNARDA

Nothing is going on.

MAGDALENA

(To ANGUSTIAS*)* If you're arguing about the inheritance— you're the richest, you keep it all.

ANGUSTIAS

Keep your tongue in its place!

BERNARDA

(Rapping the floor with her cane) Don't entertain the illusion that you are going to be a match for me! Until I leave this house feet first, I will make the decisions—my own, and yours!

(There are voices offstage and MARIA JOSEFA *enters, followed by the* MAID. BERNARDA's *mother is a very old woman, decked out with flowers on her head and at her breast)*

MARIA JOSEFA

Bernarda, where is my mantilla? I don't want any of you to have anything of mine. Not my rings or my black moiré dress. Because none of you is going to get married. Not one! Bernarda, give me my pearl necklace!

BERNARDA

(To the MAID*)* Why did you let her in?

MAID

(Trembling) She got away from me!

MARIA JOSEFA

I escaped because I want to get married, because I want to get married to a beautiful man from the edge of the sea. Since the men around here run away from women.

BERNARDA

Be quiet, Mother!

MARIA JOSEFA

No, I won't be quiet! I don't like to see these old maids, itching to get married, their hearts turning to dust. I want to go back to my own village! Bernarda, I want a man so I can get married and be happy!

BERNARDA

Lock her up!

MARIA JOSEFA

Let me come out, Bernarda!

(The MAID *takes hold of* MARIA JOSEFA*)*

BERNARDA

Help her! All of you!

(They all drag the old woman off the stage)

MARIA JOSEFA

I want to get away from here! Bernarda! To get married at the
edge of the sea, at the edge of the sea!

FAST CURTAIN

ACT II

(A white inner room in BERNARDA's *house. The doors at the left lead to the bedrooms.* BERNARDA's *daughters, except for* ADELA, *are seated in low chairs, sewing.* MAGDALENA *is embroidering.* PONCIA *is with them)*

ANGUSTIAS

I've already cut the third sheet.

MARTIRIO

It's for Amelia.

MAGDALENA

Angustias, shall I put Pepe's initials on it, too?

ANGUSTIAS

(Dryly) No.

MAGDALENA

(Calling out) Adela, aren't you coming?

AMELIA

She must be lying down.

PONCIA

Something's wrong with that girl. She seems restless, shaky, frightened—as if she had a lizard between her breasts!

MARTIRIO

There's nothing more or less wrong with her than with any of us.

MAGDALENA

All of us except Angustias!

ANGUSTIAS

I feel just fine. And anyone who doesn't like it can go to the devil!

MAGDALENA

Of course, one must admit the best things about you have always been your figure and your tact.

ANGUSTIAS

Fortunately, I'll soon be getting out of this hell!

MAGDALENA

Perhaps you won't be getting out.

MARTIRIO

Stop that talk!

ANGUSTIAS

And besides, gold in your purse is better than dark eyes in your face.

MAGDALENA

In one ear and out the other.

AMELIA

(To PONCIA*)* Open the door to the patio, to see if we can get a little fresh air.

*(*PONCIA *does so)*

MARTIRIO

Last night it was so hot I couldn't get to sleep.

AMELIA

Neither could I.

MAGDALENA

I got up to cool off. There was a black storm cloud and even a few drops of rain.

PONCIA

It was one o'clock in the morning, and the fire was rising up out of the ground! I got up, too. Angustias was still at her window with Pepe.

MAGDALENA

(Ironically) So late? What time did he leave?

ANGUSTIAS

Magdalena, why ask if you saw him?

AMELIA

He must have left about half past one.

ANGUSTIAS

Yes? How do *you* know?

AMELIA

I heard him cough, and I heard the pony stamping his hooves.

PONCIA

But I heard him leave around four o'clock.

ANGUSTIAS

That couldn't have been him.

PONCIA

I'm sure of it.

AMELIA

I thought so, too.

MAGDALENA

How very strange!

(Pause)

PONCIA

Tell me, Angustias—what did he say to you, the first time he
came to your window?

ANGUSTIAS

Nothing. What would he say to me? It was just talk.

MARTIRIO

It really is strange how two people who have never met suddenly
see each other through a window grating and—just like that—
they are engaged!

ANGUSTIAS

Well, it didn't bother me.

AMELIA

I'd feel—I don't know what.

ANGUSTIAS

Not me, because when a man approaches a window grating, he
already knows—from people who come and go, who fetch and
carry—that the answer will be yes.

MARTIRIO

Yes. But he must have asked!

ANGUSTIAS

Of course!

AMELIA

(With curiosity) And how did he ask you?

ANGUSTIAS

No special way—"You already know why I'm here, I need a
good woman, well behaved, and that's you, if you agree."

AMELIA

These things embarrass me!

ANGUSTIAS

And me. But you have to get through them.

PONCIA

Did he say any more?

ANGUSTIAS

Yes, he did all the talking.

MARTIRIO

What about you?

ANGUSTIAS

I couldn't. My heart almost jumped out of my mouth! It was the first time I was ever alone with a man at night.

MAGDALENA

And such a good-looking man!

ANGUSTIAS

He's not bad.

PONCIA

Such things are easy for people with a little experience, who talk and say things and wave their hands around. The first time my husband, Evaristo the Birdman, came to my window—ha, ha, ha!

AMELIA

What happened?

PONCIA

It was very dark. I saw him coming closer, and when he arrived, he said to me, "Good evening." "Good evening," I said to him, and we didn't speak for more than half an hour. The sweat was running down my whole body. Then Evaristo came closer and closer, as if he wanted to squeeze through the bars, and he said in a very low voice: "Come here, so I can feel you!"

(They all laugh. AMELIA *jumps up and peers out a door)*

AMELIA

Oh! I thought Mother was coming.

MAGDALENA

She would have set us straight!

(They go on laughing)

AMELIA

Sh-h-h-h . . . ! She'll hear us!

PONCIA

Afterwards, he behaved himself. Instead of doing something else, he took up breeding finches—until he died. Anyway, it's best for single women like you to know that fifteen days after the wedding a man leaves the bed for the table, then the table for the tavern. And any woman who doesn't accept it rots away crying in a corner!

AMELIA

You went along with it.

PONCIA

I could handle him!

MARTIRIO

Is it true that you hit him, sometimes?

PONCIA

Yes, and I almost put his eye out!

MAGDALENA

That's how all women should be!

PONCIA

I'm from the same school as your mother. One day he said something or other to me, and I killed all his finches with the pestle from my kitchen mortar.

(They laugh)

MAGDALENA

Adela, you shouldn't miss this!

AMELIA

Adela!

(Pause)

MAGDALENA

I'll go and see. *(Exits)*

PONCIA

That child is ill.

MARTIRIO

Of course. She hardly sleeps!

PONCIA

What does she do?

MARTIRIO

How do I know what she does!

PONCIA

You would know better than me, since you sleep with only a wall between you.

ANGUSTIAS

Envy is eating her up.

AMELIA

Don't exaggerate.

ANGUSTIAS

I see it in her eyes. She's beginning to look a little mad . . .

MARTIRIO

Don't say "mad"! This is the last place you can say that word!

(MAGDALENA *enters with* ADELA)

MAGDALENA

Well—weren't you asleep?

ADELA

I don't feel well.

MARTIRIO

(Insinuating) Didn't you sleep well last night?

ADELA

Yes.

MARTIRIO

Well, then?

ADELA

(Loudly) Leave me alone! Asleep or awake, it's none of your
business. I'll do what I want with my body.

MARTIRIO

It's only my concern for you!

ADELA

Concern? Or curiosity? Weren't you all sewing? Well, go on! I wish I were invisible, so I could walk through these rooms without being asked where I am going!

(The MAID *enters)*

MAID

Bernarda is calling you. The man who sells lace is here.

(They all exit, except PONCIA *and* ADELA. *As* MARTIRIO *leaves, she stares fixedly at* ADELA*)*

ADELA

Don't look at me anymore! If you want, I'll give you my eyes —they are brighter—and my back, to fix that crooked one of yours. But turn your head away when I go by.

*(*MARTIRIO *exits)*

PONCIA

Adela, she is your sister. Besides, she's the one who loves you the most.

ADELA

She follows me everywhere. Sometimes she peeks into my room to see if I'm asleep. She won't let me breathe! And it's always, "What a shame about that face!" "What a shame about that body, which will never belong to anyone!" No! My body will be for anyone I please.

PONCIA

(Pointedly, confidentially) For Pepe el Romano. Isn't that it?

ADELA

(Taken aback) What are you saying?

PONCIA

What I said, Adela.

ADELA

Be quiet!

PONCIA

(Loudly) Do you think I haven't noticed?

ADELA

Lower your voice!

PONCIA

Get rid of those thoughts!

ADELA

What do you know?

PONCIA

Old women can see right through the walls. Where do you go at night when you get up?

ADELA

I wish you were blind!

PONCIA

I have eyes in my head and in my hands, when it comes to things like this. No matter how much I think about it, I can't figure out what you're up to. Why were you standing at the open window, half naked, with the light burning, the second time Pepe came to talk with your sister?

ADELA

That's not true!

PONCIA

Don't be childish. Leave your sister alone; and if you want Pepe el Romano, control yourself!

(ADELA cries)

Besides, who says you can't marry him? Your sister Angustias is sickly. She won't survive her first childbirth. She's narrow in the hips, old, and from what I know, I can tell she'll die. Then Pepe will do what all widowers do in this country: he'll marry the youngest, the most beautiful, and that will be you. Live on that hope or forget him, whatever you want: just don't go against the law of God!

ADELA

Be quiet!

PONCIA

I won't be quiet!

ADELA

Mind your own business! Spy! Traitor!

PONCIA

I'll have to be your shadow.

ADELA

Instead of cleaning the house and going to bed to pray for your dead, you go sticking your nose into the affairs of men and women like an old sow, so you can slobber over them.

PONCIA

I keep watch! So people won't spit when they come through that door.

ADELA

What great affection for my sister has suddenly come over you!

PONCIA

I have no affection for any of you, but I want to live in a decent house. I don't want to be disgraced in my old age.

ADELA

Your advice is useless—it's already too late! I wouldn't fight you—you're just a servant—I'd fight my mother, to put out this fire that rises from my legs and mouth. What can you say about me? That I lock myself in my room and don't open the door? That I don't sleep? I'm smarter than you are. See if you can catch this wild rabbit with your hands!

PONCIA

Don't defy me, Adela, don't defy me! Because I can raise my voice, light the lamps, and make the bells ring!

ADELA

Bring out four thousand yellow flares and set them on the walls of the corral. No one can keep what has to happen from happening!

PONCIA

You care about him that much!

ADELA

That much! When I look into his eyes, I feel as if I am slowly drinking in his blood.

PONCIA

I can't listen to you.

ADELA

Well, you *will* listen to me! I was afraid of you. But now I'm stronger than you are.

(ANGUSTIAS enters)

ANGUSTIAS

Always arguing!

PONCIA

Of course. She insists that I go to the store in this heat to bring her I don't know what.

ANGUSTIAS

Did you buy me that bottle of perfume?

PONCIA

The most expensive. And the face powder. I put them on the table in your room.

(ANGUSTIAS *exits*)

ADELA

And keep your mouth shut!

PONCIA

We'll see about that!

(MARTIRIO, AMELIA, *and* MAGDALENA *enter*)

MAGDALENA

(To ADELA) Have you seen the lace?

AMELIA

The lace for Angustias's wedding sheets is beautiful.

ADELA

(To MARTIRIO, *who is carrying some lace)* And this?

MARTIRIO

It's for me. For a shift.

ADELA

(Sarcastically) You have to have a sense of humor.

MARTIRIO

(Pointedly) Just for me to see. I have no need to exhibit myself to anyone.

PONCIA

No one sees you in your shift.

MARTIRIO

(Pointedly, looking at ADELA*)* Sometimes! But I adore underclothes! If I were rich, mine would be made of Dutch linen. It's one of the few pleasures I have left.

PONCIA

This lace is lovely for baby bonnets and christening gowns. I was never able to use it on mine. Now we'll see if Angustias uses it on hers. If she decides to have babies, you'll all be sewing morning and night!

MAGDALENA

I don't plan to sew a stitch!

AMELIA

Much less take care of someone else's children! Just look at the women down the street, sacrificing their lives for little brats!

PONCIA

They're better off than you. At least they laugh over there, and you can hear them bashing each other around.

MARTIRIO

Then go work for *them!*

PONCIA

No. I'm stuck in this convent now.

(We hear a jingling of bells in the distance)

MAGDALENA

It's the men coming back from the fields.

PONCIA

A minute ago it struck three!

MARTIRIO

With this sun!

ADELA

(Sitting down) Oh, if only I could go out to the fields, too!

MAGDALENA

(Sitting down) Each class does what it must.

MARTIRIO

(Sitting down) That's how it is.

(AMELIA sits down with a sigh)

PONCIA

There's no greater joy than being in the fields at this time of year! Yesterday morning the harvesters arrived. Forty or fifty good-looking young men.

MAGDALENA

Where are they from this year?

PONCIA

From very far away. They came from the hills. Full of spirit! Burnt like trees. Shouting and tossing stones! Last night, a woman dressed in sequins arrived in town, and she danced to the accordion, and fifteen of them paid to take her into the olive grove. I saw them from a distance. The one who arranged it was a boy with green eyes, as tight as a sheaf of wheat.

AMELIA

Is it true?

ADELA

How can that be?

PONCIA

Years ago, another of these women came, and I myself gave
money to my oldest son so he could go. Men need these things.

ADELA

They are forgiven everything!

AMELIA

To be born a woman is the worst punishment.

MAGDALENA

And not even our eyes belong to us.

(There is singing in the distance, coming closer)

PONCIA

It's them. They have some lovely songs.

AMELIA

They're going out to harvest now.

(Offstage, tambourines and carrañacas *play. There is a pause in the
conversation; everyone listens in the sunstruck silence)*

CHORUS
(Offstage)
Harvesters going to reap the wheat,
Going in search of the golden grain.
Reaping the hearts of the girls they meet,
Hearts they will harvest again.

AMELIA

And they don't mind this sun!

MARTIRIO

They harvest right through the blazing heat.

ADELA

I'd like to be a harvester, so I could come and go. Then I could forget what's eating away at us.

MARTIRIO

What do *you* have to forget?

ADELA

Each of us has something.

MARTIRIO

(Intensely) Each of us!

PONCIA

Quiet! Quiet!

CHORUS
(At a distance)
Open your doors and your windows,
Ladies who live in this pueblo!
Harvesters beg for your roses,
Roses to trim their sombreros!

PONCIA

What singing!

MARTIRIO
(Nostalgically)
Open your doors and your windows,
Ladies who live in this pueblo!

ADELA

(Passionately)

Harvesters beg for your roses,
Roses to trim their sombreros!

(The singing fades in the distance)

PONCIA

Now they're turning the corner.

ADELA

Let's go and watch them from the window in my room!

PONCIA

Be careful not to open it too wide—they're bold enough to give
it a push to see who's looking.

*(ADELA, MAGDALENA, and PONCIA leave. MARTIRIO stays seated
in her chair with her head in her hands)*

AMELIA

(Going to her) What's the matter with you?

MARTIRIO

The heat makes me ill.

AMELIA

It's nothing more than that?

MARTIRIO

I wish November would come: the rainy days, the frost—anything but this interminable summer!

AMELIA

It will soon pass—and come again.

MARTIRIO

Of course. *(She pauses)* What time did you fall asleep last night?

AMELIA

I don't know. I sleep like a log. Why?

MARTIRIO

No reason, except I thought I heard people in the corral.

AMELIA

Yes?

MARTIRIO

Very late.

AMELIA

And you weren't afraid?

MARTIRIO

No. I've heard it before, other nights.

AMELIA

We should be careful. Could it have been the field hands?

MARTIRIO

The field hands come at six.

AMELIA

Perhaps a wild mule.

MARTIRIO

(Muttering, with a double meaning) That's it, that's it! A wild mule.

AMELIA

We have to warn the others.

MARTIRIO

No! No! Don't say anything! It could be I imagined it.

AMELIA

Perhaps.

(Pause. AMELIA *starts to exit)*

MARTIRIO

Amelia.

AMELIA

(At the door) What?

(Pause)

MARTIRIO

Nothing.

(Pause)

AMELIA

Why did you call me?

(Pause)

MARTIRIO

It slipped out. I didn't mean to.

(Pause)

AMELIA

Lie down for a while.

ANGUSTIAS

(Entering, in a rage, in great contrast to the preceding silences) Where is the picture of Pepe I had under my pillow? Which of you has it?

MARTIRIO

Neither of us.

AMELIA

It's not as if Pepe were a silver Saint Bartholomew.

(PONCIA, MAGDALENA, and ADELA enter)

ANGUSTIAS

Where is the picture?

ADELA

What picture?

ANGUSTIAS

One of you has hidden it from me!

MAGDALENA

You have the effrontery to say that?

ANGUSTIAS

It was in my room, and now it's not!

MARTIRIO

Couldn't he have slipped out to the yard in the middle of the night? Pepe likes to walk around in the moonlight.

ANGUSTIAS

Don't play tricks on me! When he comes, I'm going to tell him!

PONCIA

Don't do that; it will turn up. *(Looking at ADELA)*

ANGUSTIAS

I would like to know which of you has it!

ADELA

(Looking at MARTIRIO) Somebody! Anybody but me!

MARTIRIO

(Pointedly) Of course!

(Entering) What is all this commotion in my house, and in the
silence of this heavy heat? The neighbors must have their ears
glued to the wall!

ANGUSTIAS

They have stolen my fiancé's picture!

BERNARDA

(Fiercely) Who? Who?

ANGUSTIAS

Them!

BERNARDA

Which of you?

(Silence)

Answer me!

(Silence)

(Then, to PONCIA*)* Search the rooms, look in the beds!

*(*PONCIA *exits)*

This comes from not keeping you on a shorter leash! But I will
haunt your dreams! *(To* ANGUSTIAS*)* Are you sure?

ANGUSTIAS

Yes.

BERNARDA

Have you looked for it carefully?

ANGUSTIAS

Yes, Mother.

(They are all standing in perplexed silence)

BERNARDA

At the end of my life, you make me drink the bitterest poison a mother can swallow! *(Calling out to* PONCIA*)* Can't you find it?

PONCIA

(Entering) Here it is.

BERNARDA

Where did you find it?

PONCIA

It was . . .

BERNARDA

Don't be afraid to tell me.

PONCIA

(Surprised) Between the sheets of Martirio's bed!

BERNARDA

Is that true?

MARTIRIO

It's true.

BERNARDA

(Coming at her and hitting her with her cane) May God strike you dead, you two-faced scorpion! You troublemaker!

MARTIRIO

(Fiercely) Don't you hit me, Mother!

BERNARDA

As much as I want!

MARTIRIO

If I let you! Do you hear that? Get away!

PONCIA

Don't be disrespectful to your mother!

ANGUSTIAS

(Seizing BERNARDA*)* Leave her alone! Please!

BERNARDA

There aren't even tears left in those eyes!

MARTIRIO

I'm not going to cry just to please you.

BERNARDA

Why did you take the picture?

MARTIRIO

Can't I play a joke on my own sister? Why else would I want it?

ADELA

(Exploding with jealousy) It was not a joke—you've never liked games, never! It was something else, exploding in your heart, wanting to come out! Admit it openly, once and for all!

MARTIRIO

Be quiet, don't make me talk! Because if I talk, the walls will collapse in shame!

ADELA

A vicious tongue never stops lying!

BERNARDA

Adela!

MAGDALENA

You're both crazy!

AMELIA

And you torture us with your sinful thoughts!

MARTIRIO

Others do things that are even more sinful!

ADELA

Until they strip themselves naked, and let the river sweep them away!

BERNARDA

Shameless!

ANGUSTIAS

It's not my fault that Pepe el Romano has chosen me!

ADELA

For your money!

ANGUSTIAS

Mother!

BERNARDA

Silence!

MARTIRIO

For your fields and your orchards.

MAGDALENA

That's the truth!

BERNARDA

Silence, I said! I saw the storm coming, but I didn't think it would burst so soon. Oh, what a hailstone of hate you have flung at my heart! But I'm not old yet, and I have five chains

for you, and this house my father built, so not even the fields
will know of my desolation. Get out of here!

(They leave. BERNARDA *sits down, desolate.* PONCIA *is standing
close to the wall.* BERNARDA *collects herself and strikes the floor with
her cane)*

I must use a firm hand with them. Bernarda, remember; this is
your duty!

PONCIA

May I speak?

BERNARDA

Speak. I'm sorry you heard. It's never wise to let an outsider
into the family circle.

PONCIA

What I have seen I have seen.

BERNARDA

Angustias must get married right away.

PONCIA

Of course. We have to get her away from here.

BERNARDA

Not her. Him!

PONCIA

Of course. We must get him far away from here. Good thinking!

BERNARDA

I don't think. There are things we cannot and should not think!
I give orders.

PONCIA

And do you believe he'll want to leave?

BERNARDA

(Getting up) What's going on in that head of yours?

PONCIA

He—of course!—will marry Angustias.

BERNARDA

Go on! I know you well enough to see you already have your knife out.

PONCIA

I never thought giving a warning would be called murder.

BERNARDA

You have something to warn me about?

PONCIA

I'm not making accusations, Bernarda. I'm only telling you: open your eyes and you'll see.

BERNARDA

See what?

PONCIA

You've always been clever. You can see evil in people from a hundred miles away. I have often believed you could read people's minds. But your children are your children. And about them, you are blind.

BERNARDA

Are you referring to Martirio?

PONCIA

Well, when it comes to Martirio . . . *(With curiosity)* Why would she hide the picture?

BERNARDA

(Wanting to cover up for her daughter) After all, she says it was a joke. What else could it be?

PONCIA

(Sarcastically) Do you believe that?

BERNARDA

(Vigorously) I don't *believe* it—it is so!

PONCIA

All right—it's your family we're dealing with. But if it were the neighbor across the street—what would you think?

BERNARDA

Now you're beginning to sharpen your knife.

PONCIA

(With unrelenting cruelty) Bernarda, something monstrous is happening here. I don't want to blame you, but you haven't allowed your daughters any freedom. Martirio is romantic, no matter what you say. Why didn't you let her marry Enrique Humanas? Why did you send him a message not to come to her window, the very day he was coming?

BERNARDA

(Loud) And I would do it a thousand times again! My blood will never mix with that of the Humanas family—not as long as I live! His father was a field hand.

PONCIA

This is what comes of putting on airs!

BERNARDA

I do because I can afford to! And you don't because you know very well what you come from.

PONCIA

(With hatred) Don't remind me of that! I'm old now. I've always
been grateful for your protection.

BERNARDA

(Drawing herself up) It wouldn't seem so!

PONCIA

(With hatred masked in sweetness) Martirio will forget about this.

BERNARDA

And if she doesn't forget, the worse for her! I don't think this
is the "something monstrous" happening here. Nothing is happening here. That's what you'd like. And if something does
happen someday, rest assured it will not go beyond these walls!

PONCIA

I don't know about that—there are also people in town who can
read hidden thoughts from a distance.

BERNARDA

How you'd like to see my daughters and me on our way to the
brothel!

PONCIA

No one can know her own fate.

BERNARDA

I know my fate—and that of my daughters. We'll leave the
brothel to a certain woman who is already dead.

PONCIA

(Fiercely) Bernarda, respect the memory of my mother!

BERNARDA

Stop hounding me, you with your evil thoughts!

(Pause)

PONCIA

It's best if I don't get mixed up in anything.

BERNARDA

That's what you should do: work and keep your mouth shut. It is the obligation of those who are paid to work.

PONCIA

But I can't. Don't you think that Pepe would be better off married to Martirio or—Yes! To Adela?

BERNARDA

I do *not* think so.

PONCIA

(*Pointedly*) Adela. She's el Romano's real fiancée.

BERNARDA

Things are never the way we would like them to be.

PONCIA

But it's very hard for people to turn away from their true inclinations. For Pepe to be with Angustias seems wrong—to me, and to other people, and even to the air. Who knows if they'll get their way!

BERNARDA

Here we go again! You go out of your way to give me bad dreams. And I don't want to listen, because if things turn out the way you say they will, I'll have to claw you to pieces!

PONCIA

The blood wouldn't get as far as the river!

BERNARDA

Fortunately, my daughters respect me and have never gone against my will.

PONCIA

That's true. But as soon as you turn them loose, they'll be up on the roof.

BERNARDA

I will bring them down soon enough, by throwing stones at them!

PONCIA

Of course you are the strongest!

BERNARDA

I've always been able to hold my own.

PONCIA

But it's strange! At her age! Look at how taken Angustias is with her fiancé! And he seems to be smitten, too! Yesterday my oldest son told me that at half past four in the morning, when he went by with his oxen, they were still talking!

BERNARDA

At half past four?

ANGUSTIAS

(Entering) That's a lie!

PONCIA

That's what I was told.

BERNARDA

(To ANGUSTIAS*)* Go on!

ANGUSTIAS

For more than a week, Pepe has been leaving here at one o'clock. May God strike me dead if I'm lying!

MARTIRIO

(Entering) I heard him leave at four, too.

BERNARDA

But did you see him with your own eyes?

MARTIRIO

I didn't want to be seen. Don't you usually talk through the window facing the alley?

ANGUSTIAS

I talk through the window in my bedroom.

(ADELA appears at the door)

MARTIRIO

Then . . .

BERNARDA

What is going on here?

PONCIA

Careful, you'll find out! But it's clear Pepe was at one of the windows of your house at four in the morning.

BERNARDA

Do you know that for certain?

PONCIA

You don't know anything for certain in this life.

ADELA

Mother, don't listen to someone who wants to destroy us all!

BERNARDA

I will know how to find out. If people in this town want to bear false witness, they will find me as hard as flint. This matter is not to be discussed. Sometimes other people stir up a wave of mud in order to destroy us.

I don't like to lie.

So something *is* going on!

Nothing is going on. I was born with my eyes open. Now I'll keep watch, and never close them until I die.

I have the right to know!

You have no right except to obey! No one is going to push me around. *(To* PONCIA*)* And you take care of your own affairs. No one will take a step without my hearing it!

(Entering) There's a big crowd up the street! And all the neighbors are at their doors!

(To PONCIA*)* Run and find out what's happening!

(The women start to hurry off)

Where are you going? I always knew you were busybodies who would break your mourning. All of you, to the patio!

(They exit first, and then BERNARDA. *We hear distant voices.* MAR-TIRIO *and* ADELA *enter. They stand listening, not daring to take another step toward the outside door)*

Be grateful I didn't happen to open my mouth.

ADELA

I could have said things, too.

MARTIRIO

And what could you say? Wanting is not doing.

ADELA

She who can does—and she who takes the first step . . . You
wanted to, but you couldn't.

MARTIRIO

You won't go on like this much longer.

ADELA

I'll have it all!

MARTIRIO

I'll tear you out of his arms!

ADELA

(Pleading) Martirio, leave me alone!

MARTIRIO

Never!

ADELA

He wants me in his house!

MARTIRIO

I saw the way he embraced you!

ADELA

I didn't want to! It was like being dragged by a rope.

MARTIRIO

You'd be better off dead!

(MAGDALENA *and* ANGUSTIAS *appear. The crowd noises grow louder)*

PONCIA

(Entering with BERNARDA*)* Bernarda!

BERNARDA

What is going on?

PONCIA

Librada's daughter, the one who's not married, just had a baby, and no one knows who the father is!

ADELA

A baby?

PONCIA

And to hide her shame, she killed it and put it under some rocks. But some dogs, with more feelings than many creatures, pulled it out, and as if led by the hand of God, they put it on her doorstep. Now they want to kill her. They're dragging her down the street, and the men are running down the paths and out of the olive groves, shouting so loud the fields are trembling.

BERNARDA

Yes! Let them all bring whips made from olive branches and the handles of their hoes! Let them all come to kill her!

ADELA

No. No! Not to kill her!

MARTIRIO

Yes, let's go out there, too!

BERNARDA

Any woman who tramples on decency should pay for it!

(Outside, a woman screams, and there is a great uproar)

ADELA

They should let her go! Don't go out there!

MARTIRIO

(Looking at ADELA*)* Let her pay for what she did.

BERNARDA

(In the archway) Finish her off before the Civil Guard gets here! Burning coals in the place where she sinned!

ADELA

(Clutching her womb) No! No!

BERNARDA

Kill her! Kill her!

CURTAIN

ACT III

(The interior patio of BERNARDA*'s house. It is night. Four white walls lightly bathed in blue. The decor must be one of perfect simplicity. The doors, illuminated by the light from inside, cast a delicate glow on the scene. At center, a table with an oil lamp, where* BERNARDA *and her* DAUGHTERS *are eating.* PONCIA *is serving them.* PRUDENCIA *is seated at one side. The curtain rises on total silence, interrupted only by the clatter of dishes and cutlery)*

PRUDENCIA

I'm going now. It's been a long visit. *(She rises)*

BERNARDA

Wait, Prudencia! We never see each other.

PRUDENCIA

Has the last call for the rosary sounded?

PONCIA

Not yet.

*(*PRUDENCIA *sits down)*

BERNARDA

How is your husband getting on?

PRUDENCIA

The same.

BERNARDA

We don't see him, either.

PRUDENCIA

You know how he is. Ever since he fought with his brothers over the inheritance, he hasn't used the front door. He puts up a ladder and climbs over the wall and into the corral.

BERNARDA

He's a real man! And with your daughter?

PRUDENCIA

He has not forgiven her.

BERNARDA

He is right.

PRUDENCIA

I don't know what to tell you. I suffer because of it.

BERNARDA

A daughter who disobeys stops being a daughter and becomes an enemy.

PRUDENCIA

I just let the water flow. The only comfort I have left is to take refuge in the church, but since my eyes are failing, I'll have to stop coming, because the children tease me.

(There is a loud thud from the other side of the wall)

PRUDENCIA

What is that?

BERNARDA

The breeding stallion, locked up and kicking the wall. *(Loudly)* Shackle him and let him out in the corral! *(Confidentially)* He must be hot.

PRUDENCIA

Are you going to breed him with your new mares?

BERNARDA

At sunrise.

PRUDENCIA

You've been good at building up your herd.

BERNARDA

Thanks to money and a lot of unpleasantness.

PONCIA

(Interrupting) But she has the best herd in this part of the country. It's too bad prices are down.

BERNARDA

Would you like some cheese and honey?

PRUDENCIA

I have no appetite.

(There is another thud)

PONCIA

For God's sake!

PRUDENCIA

It made my heart pound!

BERNARDA

(Rising, furious) Must I say things twice? Let him out so he can roll around in the piles of straw. *(After a pause, as if speaking to the hired hands)* Well, shut the mares in the stable, but turn him loose before he kicks down the walls! *(She goes back to the table and sits)* Oh, what a life!

PRUDENCIA

Struggling like a man.

BERNARDA

That's the way it is.

(ADELA gets up from the table)

Where are you going?

ADELA

For a drink of water.

BERNARDA

(Calling out) Bring a pitcher of cool water! *(To* ADELA*)* You may sit down.

(ADELA sits down)

PRUDENCIA

What about Angustias, when will she get married?

BERNARDA

They are coming to ask for her hand in three days.

PRUDENCIA

You must be pleased!

ANGUSTIAS

Of course!

ADELA

(To MAGDALENA*)* Now you've spilled the salt!

MAGDALENA

Your luck can't get any worse than it is now.

AMELIA

It's always a bad sign.

BERNARDA

That's enough!

PRUDENCIA

(To ANGUSTIAS*)* Has he given you the ring yet?

ANGUSTIAS

Do look at it. *(She holds it out)*

PRUDENCIA

It's lovely. Three pearls! In my day, pearls meant tears.

ANGUSTIAS

But things have changed now.

ADELA

I don't think so. Things always mean the same. Engagement rings are supposed to be diamonds.

PRUDENCIA

It's more appropriate.

BERNARDA

With pearls or without them, things are what you make of them.

MARTIRIO

Or what God makes of them.

PRUDENCIA

Your furniture, they tell me, is lovely.

BERNARDA

I spent sixteen thousand *reales*.

PONCIA

(Interjecting) The best is the mirrored wardrobe.

PRUDENCIA

I never saw one of those fancy things.

BERNARDA

All we had was a chest.

PRUDENCIA

What's important is that things work out.

ADELA

And you never know.

BERNARDA

There's no reason why it shouldn't.

(Bells are heard, very far off)

PRUDENCIA

The last call. *(To* ANGUSTIAS*)* I'll come back soon, so you can show me the clothes.

ANGUSTIAS

Whenever you like.

PRUDENCIA

Good night. God be with you.

BERNARDA

Goodbye, Prudencia.

THE FIVE DAUGHTERS TOGETHER

God go with you.

(Pause. PRUDENCIA *leaves)*

BERNARDA

We are through eating now.

(They get up from the table)

ADELA

I'm going to the front door to stretch my legs and get a little fresh air.

(MAGDALENA sits in a low chair against the wall)

AMELIA

I'll go with you.

MARTIRIO

Me, too.

ADELA

(With repressed hatred) I'm not going to get lost.

AMELIA

You should have company at night.

(They go out. BERNARDA sits; ANGUSTIAS is clearing the table)

BERNARDA

I've already told you I want you to speak to your sister Martirio. What happened with the picture was just a joke, and you should forget it.

ANGUSTIAS

You know she doesn't love me.

BERNARDA

We each know what we're thinking inside. I don't pry into people's feelings, but I do want to keep up appearances and have harmony in the family. Do you understand that?

ANGUSTIAS

Yes.

BERNARDA
That's settled, then.

MAGDALENA
(Half asleep) Anyway, you're going to be leaving very soon! *(She falls asleep)*

ANGUSTIAS
Not soon enough, I feel!

BERNARDA
What time did you finish talking last night?

ANGUSTIAS
At half past twelve.

BERNARDA
What does Pepe have to say?

ANGUSTIAS
I find him distracted. He always talks to me as if he's thinking of something else. If I ask him what's wrong, he answers: "We men have our own worries."

BERNARDA
You shouldn't ask him. Especially after you're married. Speak if he speaks, and look at him when he looks at you. That way, you won't quarrel.

ANGUSTIAS
Mother, I think he hides many things from me.

BERNARDA
Don't try to find out about them. Don't ask him. And, above all, don't ever let him see you cry.

ANGUSTIAS
I should be happy, and I'm not.

BERNARDA

It's all the same.

ANGUSTIAS

I often stare very hard at Pepe, until he grows blurred behind the bars of the window, as if he were being covered by a cloud of dust like the sheep stir up.

BERNARDA

It's only because you're frail.

ANGUSTIAS

I hope so.

BERNARDA

Is he coming tonight?

ANGUSTIAS

No. He went to the city with his mother.

BERNARDA

Then we'll get to bed earlier. Magdalena!

ANGUSTIAS

She's asleep.

(ADELA, MARTIRIO, and AMELIA enter)

AMELIA

What a dark night!

ADELA

You can't see two steps ahead of you.

MARTIRIO

A good night for thieves, for someone who needs a hiding place.

ADELA

The stallion was in the middle of the corral—so white! Twice as big, completely filling the darkness!

AMELIA

It's true. It was frightening! It was like an apparition.

ADELA

There are stars in the sky as big as fists!

MARTIRIO

Our sister was staring so hard at them she almost broke her neck.

ADELA

Don't you like them?

MARTIRIO

I don't care what goes on above the rooftops. I have enough with what goes on inside these rooms!

ADELA

That's how you are.

BERNARDA

She has her way and you have yours.

ANGUSTIAS

Good night.

ADELA

Are you going to bed now?

ANGUSTIAS

Yes. Pepe is not coming tonight. *(She exits)*

ADELA

Mother, when there's a shooting star or a flash of lightning, why
do we say:

>Blessed Santa Barbara, why
>Are you writing, up so high,
>With holy water in the sky?

BERNARDA

In the old days they knew many things that we have forgotten.

AMELIA

I close my eyes so I won't see them!

ADELA

Not me. I like to see things blazing through the sky, after being
motionless year after year.

MARTIRIO

But these things have nothing to do with us.

BERNARDA

And it's best not to think about them.

ADELA

What a beautiful night! I'd like to stay up very late so I could
enjoy the cool air from the fields.

BERNARDA

But we have to go to bed. Magdalena!

AMELIA

She dozed off.

BERNARDA

Magdalena!

MAGDALENA

(Annoyed) Leave me in peace.

BERNARDA

Go to bed!

MAGDALENA

(Getting up peevishly) You don't leave a person alone! *(She leaves, grumbling)*

AMELIA

Good night. *(She goes)*

BERNARDA

You go, too.

MARTIRIO

Why isn't Angustias's fiancé coming tonight?

BERNARDA

He went on a trip.

MARTIRIO

(Looking at ADELA*)* Ah!

ADELA

See you in the morning.

(She leaves. MARTIRIO *drinks some water and exits slowly, looking toward the door to the corral)*

PONCIA

(Entering) Are you still here?

BERNARDA

Enjoying this silence, and unable to find any trace of that "monstrous thing" you claim is happening here.

PONCIA

Bernarda, let's forget about that conversation.

BERNARDA

In this house there is no question of "yes" or "no." My vigilance takes care of that.

PONCIA

Nothing is happening on the surface, it's true. Your daughters are tucked away in a cupboard, and that's how they live. But neither you nor anyone else can see into their hearts.

BERNARDA

My daughters breathe easily.

PONCIA

You care about that because you're their mother. For me, looking after your house is enough.

BERNARDA

Now you've decided to become silent!

PONCIA

I know my place, and I'm at peace.

BERNARDA

The trouble is, you have nothing to talk about. If there were grass growing in this house, you'd bring every sheep in the neighborhood in to graze.

PONCIA

I cover up more than you think.

BERNARDA

Does your son still see Pepe at four o'clock in the morning? Do they still tell the same malicious stories about this house?

PONCIA

They say nothing.

BERNARDA

Because they can't! Because there's no meat to bite into, thanks to my watchful eyes.

PONCIA

Bernarda, I don't want to talk, because I'm afraid of what you'll do. But don't be too sure.

BERNARDA

Absolutely sure!

PONCIA

Suddenly lightning may strike! Suddenly your heart may stop dead!

BERNARDA

Nothing is happening here! I'm quite prepared to deal with your suppositions.

PONCIA

Well, all the better for you!

BERNARDA

All the better!

MAID

(Entering) I have finished washing the dishes now. Is there anything else you want, Bernarda?

BERNARDA

(Getting up) Nothing. I'm going to bed.

MAID

What time do you want me to call you?

BERNARDA

Don't. Tonight I'm going to sleep well. *(She exits)*

PONCIA

When you can't fight the tide, it's easier to turn your back, so you don't see it.

MAID

She's so proud she puts a blindfold on herself.

PONCIA

There's nothing I can do. I tried to put a stop to all this, but now it frightens me too much. Do you hear this silence? Well, there's a storm brewing in every room. The day it bursts, we'll all be swept away! I've said what I had to say.

MAID

Bernarda thinks that no one can stand up to her. She doesn't realize the power a man can have over lonely women.

PONCIA

It's not all Pepe el Romano's fault. It's true that last year he was after Adela, and she was crazy for him. But she should have known her place and not led him on. A man is a man.

MAID

They say he spoke to Adela many nights.

PONCIA

It's true *(Lowering her voice)* And other things.

MAID

I don't know what's going to happen here.

PONCIA

I'd like to cross the ocean and get away from this house of turmoil.

MAID

Bernarda is rushing the wedding day, and perhaps nothing will happen.

PONCIA

Things have already gone too far. Adela has made up her mind to do whatever it takes, and the others keep watch, all the time.

MAID

Martirio, too?

PONCIA

She's the worst! She's a well of poison! She knows el Romano is not for her, and she would crush the world if it were in her hand.

MAID

They are wicked.

PONCIA

They are women without men, that's all. When it comes to that, you even forget your own blood. Sssssssh! *(She listens)*

MAID

What is it?

PONCIA

(Stands up) The dogs are barking.

MAID

Someone must have walked past the front door.

(ADELA enters, wearing white petticoats and a bodice)

PONCIA

Didn't you go to bed?

ADELA

I'm getting a drink of water. *(She drinks from a glass on the table)*

PONCIA

I thought you were asleep.

I woke up thirsty. And what about you, aren't you going to get some rest?

Right away.

(ADELA exits)

Let's go.

We've earned our sleep. Bernarda doesn't give me a moment's rest the whole day.

Take the lamp with you.

The dogs are barking like mad!

They're not going to let us sleep.

(They exit. The stage is almost dark. MARIA JOSEFA *enters, carrying a baby ewe, an* ovejita, *in her arms)*

> *Ovejita*, child of mine,
> Come with me to the edge of the sea.
> The little ant is at his door,
> I'll give you my breast, and bread.
>
> Bernarda—
> Face of a leopard.
> Magdalena—

Face of a hyena.
Ovejita—
Baa-baa-baa, baa-baa-baa.
We'll go to the palms at the gates of Bethlehem.

You and I don't want to sleep;
The door will open on its own
And you and I will hide ourselves
In a hut made of coral on the beach.

Bernarda—
Face of a leopard.
Magdalena—
Face of a hyena.
Ovejita—
Baa-baa-baa, baa-baa-baa.
We'll go to the palms at the gates of Bethlehem.

(She leaves, singing)

(ADELA enters. She looks furtively from side to side and disappears through the door to the corral. MARTIRIO enters through another door and stands, waiting in anguish, at the center of the stage. She, too, is in petticoats. She's wearing a black shawl with the ends tucked tightly at her waist. MARIA JOSEFA enters downstage of her)

MARTIRIO

Grandmother, where are you going?

MARIA JOSEFA

Are you going to open the door for me? Who are you?

MARTIRIO

How did you get here?

MARIA JOSEFA

I escaped. Who are you?

Go to bed.

You're Martirio, now I see you. Martirio, face of a martyr. And when are you going to have a child? I've had this one.

Where did you get that lamb?

I know it's a lamb. But why can't a lamb be a child? It's better to have a lamb than to have nothing. Bernarda, face of a leopard; Magdalena, face of a hyena.

Don't talk so loud.

It's true. Everything is very dark. Just because I have white hair you think I can't have babies. And—yes! Babies and babies and babies! This child will have white hair, and have another child, and that one, another, and all of us with hair of snow will be like the waves, one after another after another. Then we'll all settle down, and we'll all have white hair, and we'll be foam on the sea. Why isn't there any white foam here? Here there's nothing but black mourning shawls.

Be quiet, be quiet!

When my neighbor had a child, I used to take chocolate to her, and then she would bring some to me, and so on—forever and ever and ever! You will have white hair, but the neighbors won't come. I have to go, but I'm afraid the dogs will bite me. Will you come with me out to the fields? I don't like the fields. I love houses, but houses that are open, where the women are stretched out on their beds with their little children, and the men are outside, sitting on their chairs. Pepe el Romano is a giant! You all want him. But he is going to devour you, because you are grains of wheat. Not grains of wheat! Frogs without tongues!

MARTIRIO

(Emphatically) Come on. Go to bed. *(She pushes her)*

MARIA JOSEFA

Yes, but later you'll let me out, won't you?

MARTIRIO

Of course.

MARIA JOSEFA
(Weeping)
Ovejita, child of mine.
Come with me to the edge of the sea.
The little ant is at his door,
I'll give you my breast, and bread.

(MARTIRIO locks the door through which MARIA JOSEFA exited, and goes toward the door to the corral. She hesitates there, then takes two more steps)

MARTIRIO

(Quietly) Adela! *(She pauses, then goes closer to the door. Loudly)* Adela!

(ADELA appears. Her hair is a bit mussed)

ADELA

Why are you looking for me?

MARTIRIO

Stay away from that man!

ADELA

Who are you to tell me that?

MARTIRIO

That's no place for a decent woman!

ADELA

How you'd love to be there yourself!

MARTIRIO

(Loudly) The time has come for me to speak! Things can't go
on like this!

ADELA

This is only the beginning. I had the strength to go forward—
the looks and the courage you don't have! I saw death under this
roof, and I went out to look for what is mine, what belongs to
me!

MARTIRIO

That heartless man came here for someone else. You have come
between them!

ADELA

He came for the money, but his eyes were always for me.

MARTIRIO

I won't allow you to snatch him away! He is going to marry
Angustias.

ADELA

You know better than I that he doesn't love her.

MARTIRIO

I know.

ADELA

You know, because you've seen that he loves me!

MARTIRIO

(Despairing) Yes.

ADELA

(Coming close to her) He loves me! He loves me!

MARTIRIO

Stick a knife in me if you like, but don't say that to me again!

ADELA

That's why you're trying to keep me from going off with him.
You don't care if he embraces a woman he doesn't love. Me
neither. Yes, he could spend a hundred years with Angustias,
but if he embraces me, it seems terrible to you, because you love
him, too! You love him!

MARTIRIO

(Dramatically) Yes! Let me say it openly. Yes! Let my breast
explode like a bitter pomegranate! I love him!

ADELA

(Impulsively going to embrace her) Martirio, Martirio, it's not my
fault!

MARTIRIO

Don't embrace me! Don't try to soften my eyes. My blood is
no longer your blood! I try to think of you as a sister, but I see
you only as a woman! *(She pushes her away)*

ADELA

There's no solution here. If one of us has to drown, let her
drown! Pepe el Romano is mine! He takes me into the reeds at
the edge of the river!

MARTIRIO

Never!

ADELA

I can't stand the horror of this house anymore, not after knowing the taste of his mouth! I will be what he wants me to be. With the whole town against me, branding me with their fiery fingers, persecuted by people who claim to be decent, and right in front of them I will put on a crown of thorns, like any mistress of a married man!

MARTIRIO

Be quiet!

ADELA

Yes! Yes! *(Quietly)* Let's go to sleep. Let him marry Angustias. I don't care anymore. But I will go to a little house, alone, where he will see me whenever he wants, whenever he feels the need.

MARTIRIO

That won't happen as long as I have one drop of blood in my body!

ADELA

Not you—you're weak—I could bring a wild stallion to his knees with the strength in my little finger!

MARTIRIO

Don't raise your voice, I can't stand it! My heart is full of something so vicious I can't keep it from smothering me!

ADELA

They teach us to love our sisters. God must have abandoned me out in the middle of the darkness, because I see you as if I had never seen you before!

(A whistle is heard. ADELA *runs toward the door, but* MARTIRIO *blocks it)*

Where are you going?

Get away from the door!

Get past if you can!

Get away! *(They struggle)*

(Loudly) Mother! Mother!

(BERNARDA appears, in petticoats and a black shawl)

Stop it! Stop it! How poor I am, with no bolt of lightning between my fingers!

(Pointing at ADELA) She was with him! Look at her petticoats, covered with straw!

That is the bed of sinful women! *(She moves toward ADELA, furious)*

(Confronting her) The shouting in this prison is over! *(She seizes her mother's cane and breaks it in two)* This is what I do with the tyrant's rod! Don't take one step more. No one gives me orders but Pepe!

(Entering) Adela!

(PONCIA *and* ANGUSTIAS *enter*)

ADELA
I am his woman. *(To* ANGUSTIAS*)* Get that into your head—and go out to the corral and tell him. He will be master of this entire house! He's out there, breathing like a lion!

ANGUSTIAS
My God!

BERNARDA
The gun! Where is the gun?

(She runs out, followed by MARTIRIO. AMELIA *appears upstage, looking on in terror, her head against the wall.* MARTIRIO *follows)*

ADELA
No one is going to stop me! *(She starts to leave)*

ANGUSTIAS
(Seizing her) You're not leaving here—you and your triumphant body! Thief! You're a dishonor to our house!

MAGDALENA
Let her go some place we'll never see her again.

(A shot is heard)

BERNARDA
(Entering) I dare you to find him now!

MARTIRIO
(Entering) That's the end of Pepe el Romano!

ADELA
Pepe! My God! Pepe! *(She runs out of the room)*

PONCIA

Did you kill him?

MARTIRIO

No. He ran off on his horse.

BERNARDA

It was not my fault. A woman is not trained to use a gun.

MAGDALENA

Then why did you say that?

MARTIRIO

Because of her. I would have poured a river of blood over her head!

PONCIA

Damn you!

MAGDALENA

You're a fiend!

BERNARDA

Though it's better this way.

(There is a heavy thud)

Adela! Adela!

PONCIA

(At the door) Open up!

BERNARDA

Open up! Don't think these walls can hide your shame!

MAID

(Entering) The neighbors are awake!

BERNARDA

(Like the low roar of a lion) Open up, or I'll break down the door!
(She pauses. All is silent) Adela! *(She backs away from the door)*
Bring a hammer!

*(*PONCIA *shoves the door open and enters. Then she screams and runs out)*

What is it?

PONCIA

(Her hands at her throat) God keep us from coming to that end!

(The sisters draw back from the door. The MAID *crosses herself.*
BERNARDA *screams and steps forward)*

PONCIA

Don't go in!

BERNARDA

No. Not me! Pepe, you may go running off alive, through the
shadows of the poplars, but one day you will fall. Cut her down.
My daughter has died a virgin. Carry her to her room and dress
her in white. No one is to say a thing. She died a virgin. Send
word for the bells to toll twice at dawn.

MARTIRIO

She was fortunate a thousand times over—she had him.

BERNARDA

I want no weeping. We must look death in the face. Silence! *(To
another daughter)* Be quiet, I said! *(To another daughter)* Tears,
when you're alone. We will all drown ourselves in a sea of
mourning. The youngest daughter of Bernarda Alba has died a
virgin. Did you hear me? Silence! Silence, I said! Silence!

CURTAIN

TRANSLATOR'S NOTE

MUSIC

Translator's Note

Carmen Zapata and I began to translate Lorca's plays in 1977, not by choice but of necessity. Carmen was spending her off-camera hours creating a new Los Angeles theater company, the Bilingual Foundation of the Arts, a group which performed with the actors playing their roles one night in Spanish and the next in English. Carmen was eager to get her teeth into the extraordinary repertory of feminine roles in the Lorca canon, but there were no translations that she felt were playable.

So we set to work to make a translation of *Bodas de sangre* that would be accepted by bilingual actors and audiences. In four weeks we gave the actors our "final" draft. What a revelation! Immersed in the original, the actors had all sorts of problems with our translation. They were thinking and feeling in Spanish, but were being asked to speak in English. When good actors just couldn't force out our words, we knew that changes were called for. Hundreds of changes, from single words to complete sentences. Occasionally, the actors themselves could tell us what was needed. More often, we had to be there at the moment when they stumbled, then talk to them during a rehearsal break, retire to the lobby to talk through our own solution, and then scribble away in our seats, rewriting and rewriting.

The process continued all the way through *Blood Wedding*'s two-month run. After closing night, we began our own work sessions, preparing a new draft for yet another kind of script tryout. This time we would mount an English-only staged reading, casting monolingual actors who didn't know the original. And we would give performances for English-only audiences. By then we both knew that we'd stumbled onto something—a way to forge play translations out of the long process of readings and tryouts and rewrites, that series of crucibles from which original scripts emerge as playable dramas. As master translator Gregory Rabassa once told me, "Good dialogue is like a good pair of boots: it takes a little spit to make them shine." Over the years we further revised *Blood Wedding*, and went through much the same process with *Yerma* and *The House of Bernarda Alba*, until we began work on a second set of Lorca's plays.

Many people encouraged us in our work. The playwright's sister,

Isabel García Lorca, and his nephew, Manuel Fernández-Montesinos, expressed their interest in having better English translations of these plays, and gave their authorization to these versions. The National Endowment for the Arts and the Del Amo Foundation, Los Angeles, provided funding. Christopher Maurer checked our original against reliable Spanish editions of these plays (Mario Hernández, ed., *Obras*, Madrid, Alianza Editorial, 1981 ff.), and made a number of suggestions. This edition has been thoroughly revised since its original appearance (*The Rural Trilogy*, Bantam Books, 1987). Our *Blood Wedding* won a cornucopia of awards in its 1984 revival, and *Yerma* was given a 1983 Drama-logue Award for stage writing, the first time a translation had won it. I trust that our approach—continuous revision, tried out with live actors—is consistent with Lorca's vision of theater as a "live" (rather than bookish) phenomenon which evolves *onstage*. When an Italian journalist asked him in 1935 whether or not he intended to publish his works, he broke into laughter.

Publish? I don't publish my plays. I have them recited and performed. Plays are made to be felt in the theater. They should last as long as the performance does, that's enough. If the audience wants to see them again, they can come back to life, one time or twenty, or fifty, but that is that. This is what makes the theater so lovely: as soon as it is created, it disappears.

My dearest hope is that reading and seeing Lorca in English will encourage people to read his poems and see his plays in their incomparable original.

Michael Dewell
Los Angeles

Music

BLOOD WEDDING

Music given by Lorca to Irene Lewisohn for the New York premiere of *Bodas de sangre* (*Bitter Oleander*) at the Neighborhood Playhouse, February 1935, and used in Spanish productions during the author's lifetime. Copyist unknown. Manuscript from the Billy Rose Theatre Collection, New York Public Library. The Neighborhood Playhouse performance also made use of the *Canciones populares españolas* recorded by García Lorca (piano) and Encarnación López Júlvez, "La Argentinita."

1. Lullaby of the horse, Act I, Scene 2 (p. 17). Based on a traditional Spanish cradle song, which Lorca discusses at length in his lecture "On Lullabies."

2. Epithalamium, Act II, Scene 1 (p. 42): Literally, "Let the bride awaken, / the morning of the wedding." Voice, guitar, castanets, and tambourines.

3. Bridal entourage, Act II, Scene 1 (p. 55): "On leaving your house, / Maiden so pure, / Remember: you leave / Like a star!" Voice, guitar, castanets, tambourines.

4. The servant's song, Act II, Scene 2 (p. 58): "Turning— / The wheel was turning . . ."

5. Spinning song, Act III, Scene 2 (p. 94): "Two GIRLS dressed in dark blue are unwinding a red *madeja*, a skein of wool. A LITTLE GIRL watches."

6. Chant for women mourners, Act III, Scene 2. Lorca has titled this piece "Viejo romance infantil" (Old Children's Ballad), as though he had used a traditional ballad. See "Introduction," p. xvi.

Music from *Yerma*, reprinted from Mario Hernández, Madrid, Alianza Editorial, 1981. In an interview in 1934, Lorca remarks that in the "outdoor scenes" (which include songs 3 and 4) "the protagonists have no role at all; the only actors are authentic choruses in the Greek manner. These choruses, which I began [using] in *Blood Wedding*—with the timidity of a first experience, in [Act II, Scene 1]—acquire, in *Yerma*, greater relevance and importance and a more intense development."

1. Lullaby, Act I, Scene 1 (p. 111): Literally, "Lullaby. We will make a little hut in the countryside, and stay inside it." Lorca makes use of a traditional cradle song from Guadix, which he had praised in his lecture "On Lullabies."

2. Song of the shepherd, Act I, Scene 2 (p. 132), imitative of traditional folksongs in which a maiden addresses a shepherd or complains about having to sleep alone.

3. Song of the washerwomen, Act II, Scene 1 (p. 138): "In the icy stream, / I wash your sash. / Warmer than a jasmine / Is your laugh."

4. Song of the pilgrimage, Act III, Scene 2 (p. 174): "I couldn't see you, / When you were single, / But now that you're married / I will find you."

"Song of the Reapers" from Act II of *The House of Bernarda Alba*, written by Ian Krouse, who adapted it from a Spanish folksong. Used in National Repertory Theatre/Bilingual Foundation of the Arts productions.